The Good Stripper

THE GOOD STRIPPER

A Soccer Mom's Memoir of Lies, Loss and Lapdances

MARCI WARHAFT

sh.
SUTHERLAND
HOUSE
TORONTO, 2020

Sutherland House
416 Moore Ave., Suite 205
Toronto, ON M4G 1C9

First edition, September 2020

If you are interested in inviting one of our authors to a live event or
media appearance, please contact publicity@sutherlandhousebooks.com
and visit our website at sutherlandhousebooks.com for more
information about our authors and their schedules.

Manufactured in the United States
Cover designed by Lena Yang
Book composed by Karl Hunt

Library and Archives Canada Cataloguing in Publication
Title: The good stripper : a soccer mom's memoir of lies,
loss and lapdances / Marci Warhaft.
Names: Warhaft, Marci, author.
Identifiers: Canadiana 20200283715 |
ISBN 9781989555347 (softcover)
Subjects: LCSH: Warhaft, Marci. |
LCSH: Stripteasers—Biography. |
LCGFT: Autobiographies.
Classification: LCC PN1949.S7 W37 2020 |
DDC 792.702/8092—dc23

ISBN 978-1-989555-34-7

CONTENTS

AUTHOR'S NOTE:

I have done my best to be honest and faithful to facts in telling the story that follows. The names and details of some family members have been withheld to protect their privacy, and the names of others have been changed for the same reason.

Marci Warhaft, Toronto

For anyone who may be struggling with forgiving themselves for the mistakes they made when they were just doing their best to survive.

ACKNOWLEDGEMENTS

A massive thank you to Ken Whyte/ Sutherland House, for believing that my story was one worth sharing and for letting me tell it my way. Your insight and guidance were indispensable.

Thank you to Lena Yang for a cover design that is better than anything I could have imagined.

Thank you, Matthew Bucemi for your book edits and for being so great at easing my worries along the way.

Thank you, Sarah Miniaci for your promotional expertise. I am truly grateful to be working with you.

Thank you, Rebecca Eckler, for taking the time to encourage my dream and help make it happen. I'll be forever grateful.

Thank you, Tish Cohen, for seeing the uniqueness in my story and for fanning the flame that was flickering.

Thank you, Myra Giberovitz, for your editing and organizational skills and for cheering me on through the beginning process.

To my tribe . . .

Stephanie Davis Don, thank you for treating me like family, dishing out tough love when it was warranted and walking with me step by step, word by word.

Lisa Goodman, thank you for consistently encouraging me to write this book. I finally did it! Thank you for loving me when I felt the most unlovable.

Reesa Cohen, thank you for having my back in Vancouver and being an amazing friend throughout the years that followed.

Mickey Held, we bonded in the eighth grade and have had each other's backs ever since. A friendship like ours is rare. Thank you.

Andrea Donsky, the world is a better place because of women like you who support other women in reaching their goals. Thank you for always believing in me.

Lori Mayne, we've been sisters all our lives, but only became friends while I was writing this book. Thank you for being the fierce to my feisty. Mom and Billy would be so proud.

To my boys, I hope above everything else you understand how much I adore you and how proud I am of the men you're becoming. Thank you for appreciating my free-spirited ways, even when you didn't fully understand them. I gave you life, but being your mom saved mine. Dream big, boys, dream big!

To my mother, Shirley Mayne and my brother, Billy Warhaft, thank you for your unconditional love and selfless protection every day that I had you, and for continuing to watch over me after you were taken too soon. My heart still hurts from missing you, but I know that I was incredibly lucky to have you at all.

INTRODUCTION

Cassidy in Command

"**G**ENTLEMEN! Put your hands together and welcome Cassidy to the stage!"

I take a deep breath as the pumping beat of Destiny's Child's "Bootylicious" pours through the speakers.

Wearing a black lace teddy that fits my body perfectly, I strut onto the stage. My curls are wild, my lips cherry red. I start dancing and immediately find myself agreeing with Beyoncé and the girls: "I don't think they *are* ready for this jelly."

I'm surprisingly good at this, considering how new I am. I've always loved dancing and have never been shy about moving my body in front of an audience. Of course, this is a far cry from dance recitals at summer camp. And it's worlds away from ballet class where I got kicked out, at age seven, for moving my hips and shoulders too much. "Too much wiggling, not enough discipline!" my instructor said. She wasn't wrong, and she'd be very disappointed to see me now, but *this* is exhilarating.

I move to the front of the stage and swing my hips from side to side while scanning the roomful of strangers looking up at me. The second song starts: "Dirrrrrty" by Christina Aguilera. Time to take something off. That's the rule, by the way. First song, clothes stay on. Second song, top comes off. By the middle of the third song . . . naked.

I run my hands along my hips until the tips of my fingers grasp the bottom of my teddy and slowly slip it over my head, exposing my red bra and thong. I tilt my head to the side and bite my lower lip while I unhook my bra, never losing eye contact with the fortyish-looking gentleman sitting alone to the side of the stage.

He likes me, I can tell.

I like to make a connection with one man in the audience. It's my hook. I make him feel special so that when I get off stage, I can approach him more easily for private dances. This guy hasn't taken his eyes off me since he sat down. His bushy beard and messy hair make me think of comedian Zach Galifianakis. "Ok, Zach," I think to myself, "You're mine now."

One last song – "One Last Breath," by Creed – and then I gather up my clothes, giving one last coy look to the crowd before I head backstage. I quickly change into outfit number two, a slinky red negligee, easy to take on and off. I grab my shake. Some of my co-workers indulge in lines of coke and shots of Tequila, but I've got the low-fat, high-protein power shake my trainer makes me drink every six hours.

I met my trainer, Buff Bobby, at the twenty-four-hour gym I joined a month ago. My eating disorder is in high gear right now, which means I'm under-eating, over-training and barely sleeping. Which also means I'm easy pickings for a money-hungry trainer.

"I can make you look like a fitness model!" Bobby announced as he approached me one day at the weight rack. He told me about an intense workout program he had developed that could completely transform my body in two months, if I followed it exactly. He warned me that it involved extreme dieting and hardcore training. It was not for amateurs.

"Hell, yeah!" I said. Extreme dieting was hardly a deterrent for me, and I so badly wanted the improvements. Never mind that I had almost died just four years earlier, and it had taken months for me to learn how to eat, walk, and even breathe again on my own. In the end, my eating disorder made sure I cared more about looking fit than being healthy.

"I'll do whatever it takes," I assured him.

What it took, it turned out, was money. My boys were still toddlers, and I was a stay-at-home mom. It always felt wrong to take money from my family when I wasn't contributing financially. I needed to find a job that would allow me to be at home with my kids all day, tuck them into bed at night, and be there when they woke up in the morning. That is where Cassidy came in.

I'm pretty sure the average soccer mom would not have come up with stripping as a solution but, let's face it, I'm not the average soccer mom. At the point Buff Bobby approached me, my marriage was in a rough patch and I was convinced I served only two purposes: homemaker and sex toy. It took years of his subtle manipulation, plus a near death experience, the deaths of my mother, father, brother, and multiple miscarriages to bring me to the double life I'm leading today: Marci, thirty-four-year-old housewife by day, and Cassidy, twenty-eight-year-old stripper by night.

To be fair, my husband wasn't thrilled when I told him about my plan, but not because he had an issue with me being naked in front of strange men. It was because he had an issue with me being naked in front of strange men who he hadn't chosen for me. The man I had married was not the strait-laced individual I'd thought he was. He had a controlling side, and he could be manipulative, although he didn't show much of this until four years after we'd exchanged our vows, after I lost my mom to breast cancer and eight months after my son had been delivered premature.

"If you could have sex with one of my friends, who would it be?" he asked when we were in bed one night.

"Um, none of them," I answered honestly.

"But if you *had* to, who would you choose?" he asked again.

"Why would I have to have sex with one of your friends?" I asked.

"You wouldn't. I just think it would be kinda cool to watch you have sex with someone."

I have to stop here for a second and tell you that I am far from prudish, especially these days. It wasn't the notion of another man that took me aback. But, for Christ's sake, my mother had just died and we had almost lost our son due to complications. Could there have possibly been a worse time to talk about lending out my pussy for his pleasure?

The conversation ended there but came up again, several times, over the next couple of years. He stopped while I was hospitalized for two months with a life-threatening bacterium. A year after I had recovered, however, he jumped back into it. I had just given birth to our second son.

"Let's take some pictures," he said one night after both boys were in bed. He had borrowed the digital camera from work.

"Let's take some hot pictures, just for us," he pleaded, barely containing a giddy smile.

I was a bit embarrassed by the whole thing but he was really excited, so I agreed. Wanting to leave nothing to the imagination, my husband gave the camera an in-depth view of my lady parts that only my gynecologist had ever shared. After our little porn-shoot, he told me about a website that lets you upload naked pictures of yourself for strangers to comment and rate. He suggested we do that with mine.

"Are you shitting me?" I said.

I wasn't ashamed of my body but I was creeped out by the lack of control I'd have over who was looking at me naked.

Three weeks later, my husband came home from work and as I was setting the table for dinner, he whispered in my ear: "Just so you know, I posted the pictures."

Before I could say anything, he giggled and told me that "an email went around the office today reminding everyone who borrows the camera for personal use to delete the pictures before returning it."

Oh my god.

He had posted my pictures online for strangers to see and left them on the camera for his co-workers to see. There isn't a strong enough word to describe how betrayed I felt. And alone. And unprotected.

I don't believe his motives were sinister. In his eyes, it was just naughty fun. I guess that was understandable because I had agreed to show off my body. But it still felt horrible. Then came the confusing part.

"You're getting rave reviews on the website," he said.

Damn it. He was counting on the positive feedback from men on the website to convince me that what he'd done was okay, and I shouldn't feel betrayed. I looked at the comments and while part of me was still mortified by what he had done, the compliments were gratifying.

"I knew you'd be okay with it," he said.

Was I?

I felt like I was going a little crazy. After my last pregnancy, I had started to feel unusual. It didn't feel like post-partum depression. In fact, if there was a condition that was the complete opposite of that, I had it. I felt empowered, hypersexual, and full of energy. Sounds great, but it wasn't. I was off kilter, not thinking clearly, and extremely exploitable. Years later, it would be explained to me as "traumatic overload." Basically, after years' worth of trauma and hurtful behavior from my husband, my mind was checking out. It was a form of self-preservation. While I felt madly in love with my children and protective of them, I felt disconnected from myself. I started seeing my body the same way my husband did: as a toy, and he was more than ready to enjoy the benefits of it.

He chose the friend he wanted me to have sex with. I still didn't want to do it, especially since the guy he picked was an idiot, but I found it more and more difficult to say no. My husband had purposely chosen this guy because he knew how much I disliked him, so he didn't see him as a threat. We arranged for him to come over one night when the kids were asleep and then Idiot and I started having sex while my husband watched. Then it was my husband's turn to have sex with me while Idiot watched. The lowest point for me came when they high-fived each other in the middle of everything. Suddenly, I felt like a drunk sorority girl, getting double teamed by a couple of frat brothers. I felt betrayed again.

The tables were turned when Idiot started calling me behind my husband's back. We met again, secretly, just the two of us. Don't get me wrong. He was still an Idiot, but as stupid as this probably sounds, I needed to have sex with him on *my* terms. The only winner in this scenario was Idiot, who got to fuck me twice. My self-worth was taking a dive. Yet my self-confidence around my appearance was soaring.

My husband suggested we start going to strip bars and it became a regular thing for us. Not your typical date night, that's for sure. For him, he got to see naked women. For me, I got to feel like I was in control of the situation. Our routine was simple. He'd sit at a table, while I'd look for a dancer who he'd find attractive. I'd approach her and give her $60, enough money for three dances. Two dances weren't worth her time off the floor, but more than three would be excessive because we did have a babysitter to pay for. They'd go off to a private room while I'd sit at the table and watch the show. I felt like a boss. The women loved me, because they could chat with me without having to worry that I'd try to stick my fingers where they didn't belong.

Our favorite club was a rowdy place where a dancer would pull women from the crowd onto the stage. The women would flash their boobs and the crowd would go wild. I'd been on that stage more times than I can remember, but instead of flashing my boobs, I'd let the dancers strip me naked. It was only for a few seconds, but it was a rush. It was also extremely risky because the bar wasn't far from where we lived and there was always the chance of being seen by someone I knew, but it didn't feel real. It felt like I was playing a role in a movie where the director never yelled "cut!"

One night, we were sitting by the stage and my husband whispered to me, "Go up, get naked and dance for everyone." So, I did. I crawled onto the stage, stripped off my dress and actually danced for half a song. When I was done, I was excited to hear huge praise from my husband about how amazing and brave I was, but felt horribly deflated when he said, "It would have been so much hotter had you laid down, spread eagle on the floor in front of everyone." Ugh.

I was never enough for my husband. He kept wanting more, and he always seemed to be setting the terms. After our experience with Idiot, he still wanted me to sleep with other people and he started researching fetish and swinger clubs and parties.

With all of the public nudity I was going to be engaging in, the pressure to be thin was heavy. That's why it was so important for me to accept Buff Bobby's training offer. Once my husband realized that working as a dancer meant I could also pay our grocery bills, he jumped on board. He even took me to my audition. We picked a club that was far from where we lived. I stepped on stage and did my best stripper imitation to "Slave 4 U" by Britney Spears. I felt calm and fearless. The whole traumatic overload thing was like a giant sedative. I didn't feel anxious about things that should have scared or upset me. On my way out of the audition, I was given the greenlight to be a freelancer. I wasn't a scheduled performer, so I could just show up whenever it suited me.

Which brings me here, to this club, about to approach Mr. Galifianakis and charm him into paying me to dance on his lap. This was the part I hated the most: selling myself. Stripping in public? That was easy. But having to sit with some guy and try to convince him to pay me to get naked was humiliating. "Hi, I'm Cassidy!" I said with my huge smile on my face as I sat down next to him.

"I'm Zach," he said shyly.

My brain shouted to me: "Shut up! That is not his real name!"

The server comes over and I order a "Tropical Special," which is code for non-alcoholic. It's just orange juice with cherries in it. This is the club rule: if we're offered a drink, we have to take it, and if it's not alcoholic, we need to pretend otherwise. The Tropical Special . . . none of the alcohol, all of the price!

Zach works in marketing, for some company I've never heard of. He's married. That's all I get. Zach isn't chatty and, unfortunately for me, he's cheap. The dude buys one dance. One! Even I used to buy my husband three. I just want to get through the song and move on to someone else. Wait! Is that your hand on my ass, Zach? "No touching, big guy. Sorry," I say as I remove said hand from my glutes. Song's over. See ya.

Three young guys wave me over to their table. I'd guess they're in their late twenties and not nearly as cute as they think they are. I'm going to have my hands full with this group. They want six dances in total. I start doing my thing but end up spending most of my time swatting their hands from my crotch. They think they're hilarious, but I'm getting annoyed. One of the bouncers comes over and threatens to kick them out if they don't keep their hands to themselves.

"Which one of us is the hottest?" the chubby one asks me.

"The one who's paying," I say with a smirk.

"Oh, she's smart!" He seems surprised.

The sixth song is finally over and with my money in his hand, the leader of the group says, "How about you come back to our hotel for a little fun?"

He says fun. I hear rape and murder. "No thank you, I'm good!"

Okay, who's next? I see Keith. He is one of the club's regulars, sitting in the VIP lounge. He just celebrated his sixtieth birthday and is going through a nasty divorce. Keith appreciates the company of young, beautiful women and is willing to pay for it. A week ago, he asked me if I'd be his girl-on-call. The expectation would be for me to be his companion whenever he needed one. It wasn't a sugar daddy situation, just a pay-as-you go thing. I'll be honest with you: Cassidy was tempted. A decent guy, willing to pay me for something I do for free anyway? It wasn't as easy to turn down as it should have been. Cassidy would have done the deal, but Marci had two babies at home and she decided they were the only people she'd be on call for.

Which reminds me, I need to pick up cupcakes for my son's daycare tomorrow.

"Cassidy!" Keith calls out, "join us!" He introduces me to Jim, an unhappily married father of three teenagers who doesn't want to go home. Keith pays me for six dances and tells me to take care of him.

I spend the next twenty-four minutes writhing and rolling my body over and around Jim's. He's not allowed to touch me, but I can grind my ass up and down his crotch and slide my hands along his thighs, stopping just before reaching his package. There's something empowering about knowing that you've got a man completely excited and he can't do anything about it. I'm being super flirty, giving him a playful smile while looking right into his eyes. He's loving it and so am I. I like making men feel good. I like feeling that men want me and are desperate to have me. Lately, I've been craving it. If my husband is fine with me having sex with other men when he's around, than he shouldn't really care if I start branching out on my own. If he won't appreciate me, then I'll find men who do.

It's the end of our dances and the end of the night. I say my goodbyes, grab my stuff from my locker, tip the DJ, and head home. It's 3:30 a.m.

I'll get home by 4 a.m., eat my trainer-approved snack of half a piece of baked chicken and a few green beans, and then get to the gym by 5 a.m. After a two-hour workout, I'll go to the grocery store to pick up some cupcakes and get home before the boys wake up.

Time for Cassidy to sleep, and Marci to take over.

That was the treadmill I was on, my double life, flitting between two worlds and telling myself it was normal. Strangely enough, part of me was fine with my stripper life; I was having fun and taking pleasure in the empowerment it brought me, and I definitely needed the money. But then again, it had had taken a lot of bad shit to bring me to a place where I could find refuge in being a stripper. Where being on stage as Cassidy was about the only place that I felt strong and protected. Where sexual adventures, even if harmful or degrading, were the only ways for me to experience self-worth. This was all the result of the traumatic overload that I had experienced.

Another part of me knew I was out of control, that my lifestyle wasn't what I wanted or needed for myself. In my less manic hours, I knew it was unsustainable. The lines between naughty vixen and suburban housewife were starting to blur. It couldn't end well.

Cassidy was telling me it would all somehow work out, and she was in charge most of the time. She could rationalize my bad decisions. She convinced me that she was my best option or, at least, that I had no other options. So, I stayed in the Cassidy zone, managing as best I could. I was stuck. Whoever I used to think I was, or had ever dreamed of becoming, was gone and barely remembered.

As it turned out, I couldn't make it all work. It wasn't long before the euphoria I had once felt in this double life evaporated and I was fantasizing about driving my car into a concrete abutment after dropping the kids at school. It was the only escape I could imagine.

PART ONE

THINGS THAT MAKE YOU WHO YOU ARE

CHAPTER ONE

Marci

"YOU'RE JUST FULL OF PISS and vinegar, aren't you?" my father asked as I stomped into the living room and threw my schoolbag on the sofa.

"What? That's gross!" I responded.

"What's wrong, did you have a bad day at school?" my mother asked.

It had actually started as a good day. As usual, my third-grade classmates had waited until I got there to start our morning game of freeze tag. At the beginning of the school year, it had been established that our daily schoolyard games wouldn't start until either Joanna or I were there to take the lead. Joanna and I were both athletic, confident, hyper-competitive eight-year-olds and natural leaders. I was spunky and, I think, nicer. She was much smarter. She was the smartest kid I knew. While the rest of my friends and I were reading *Superfudge* by Judy Blume, Joanna was breezing through Leon Uris' *Exodus*.

That morning, after a particularly spirited game of tag, I walked into French class ready to get to work. Unfortunately, but not surprisingly, my teacher, Monsieur Grouch, was not in a teaching mood. He never was.

Monsieur G liked to yell. The yelling was unpleasant but it was the violence that upset me. Monsieur G saved his physical aggression for a specific group of boys. I knew these boys as Sam, Scott, and Marcus, but to Monsieur G they were "*Les singes sauvages*" or the wild monkeys. They were always punished for misbehaving, even when they were doing exactly what the rest of us were doing. Monsieur G chased them around the room and threw books at them on a daily basis. Watching this was difficult. I'd shout, "Stop!" He'd scream, "*Tais-toi!*" telling me to shut up.

On this particular day, Monsieur G seemed more agitated than usual. Halfway through the period, from the corner of my eye, a crumpled piece of paper flew through the air and just missed the garbage can by the blackboard. It was Scott. Scott had crumpled the paper into a makeshift basketball and missed his target. The wad bounced onto the floor in front of Monsieur G's desk. Monsieur G lifted his eyes from his newspaper, looked at the crumpled ball on the floor, stood up, and slammed both of his hands on his desk.

"*Qui a fait cela?*" his voice boomed.

He was asking who threw it. None of us said a word.

Eventually, Scott, from behind me, said, "Me, I did it. I'm sorry, I was trying to . . ."

He started to explain that he was aiming for the garbage can but stopped talking when Monsieur G charged at him. Scott ran to the back of the room and Monsieur G was right behind him. He grabbed Scott by the shirt with both hands and threw him up against the wall, holding him there for what felt like forever. When he finally let him down, he ordered Scott to sit in the corner of the room for the rest of the period.

Scott sat there, head in his hands, crying. I started crying too, partly out of empathy for Scott and partly out of anger towards Monsieur G. I knew what I'd seen was wrong. I was furious and I felt helpless. As soon as the school bell rang, I raced home. I needed to talk to my mom.

When I stomped into the living room, I was surprised to see my father. He ran a jewelry business and was rarely home before 6:30 p.m. I assumed he had taken the afternoon off. I told my parents about French class and explained how angry I was. My father said, "If you're that upset about it, why don't you circulate a petition about him?"

"What's a petition?" I asked. He said he was being sarcastic and didn't think I should write one. My mom, however, thought it was a good idea and explained petitions to me.

The idea that I could write something that could possibly change the way Monsieur G was treating us was exciting to me. "I'm on it!" I yelled, and ran upstairs to my bedroom to get started.

I wrote about how Monsieur G made us feel and what he needed to do to be a better teacher.

1. Less yelling
2. No violence
3. Be nicer to the boys and stop calling them monkeys
4. Teach us something

I made it clear that I was not trying to get him into trouble. I just wanted his students to feel safe in class. Once I felt confident about what I had created, I left space at the bottom of the page for everyone to sign. I fell asleep that night feeling impressed with myself.

Morning did not come soon enough. I started circulating the petition as soon as I got to school. My classmates were eager to sign and show their support. All but Joanna. She was my best friend and co-leader on the playground, but she was the only person in my entire class who refused to sign. Joanna said that it was a waste of time.

"Do you really think the principal is gonna give a crap about what you think?"

"I don't know, but I have to try," I told her.

Joanna went on to become a successful corporate lawyer, to no one's surprise.

A couple of minutes before the morning school bell rang, I went to the office and handed the secretary my petition: a single, handwritten page of grade school revolt. I walked into my first class of the day and waited.

Two hours later, a voice came over the classroom intercom asking me and the first three students whose names were on my petition to go to the office to meet with the vice principal. We looked at each other with trepidation, got up, and went to the office. Were we in trouble? Had they called our parents? Were we getting suspended?

Standing in the vice principal's office, I felt like a criminal in a police lineup. We were instructed to keep our eyes facing front and not to speak to one another. He wanted details. Very specific details. He didn't just want to know that Monsieur G chased the boys around our classroom. He wanted exact dates and times. I began to resent the tone of his questions. I also felt badly for the three students who were being interrogated with me. The petition was my idea and now they were being yelled at and pressured to give details we weren't entirely sure about. This was not how I imagined things would happen.

"You are making some very serious accusations. Are you sure you're telling the truth?" the vice principal pressed us.

"Yes," we all answered.

"Thank you, you may go." He pointed to the door.

We left feeling shell-shocked as well as disappointed. I had hoped to save the day and instead found myself hoping I hadn't traumatized my friends. At lunchtime in the schoolyard, our friends swarmed around, asking a million questions. I was deflated and a little embarrassed to tell them it had all been a waste of time. I have to give Joanna credit. The grin on her face showed how desperately she wanted to say "I told you so" . . . but she didn't.

After school, over chocolate fudge cake and a glass of milk, I told my mom what happened and how disappointed I was. She was furious about how we were treated, but proud of me for speaking up.

A few hours later, the phone rang. It was the principal of my school.

"Is this Marci?" he asked.

"Yes," I answered.

Mr. Principal explained that he had read my petition and was upset by it. He told me that he had spoken to Monsieur G, who promised that things would improve immediately. Then the principal thanked me for bringing everything to his attention and apologized for the fact that I had to take these steps to bring everything to light.

I was floored. But the surprises didn't end there. Next, he put Monsieur G on the phone. It was his turn to apologize. His words were spoken so softly, I barely recognized his voice. Monsieur G asked me to put my parents on the phone so he could apologize to them as well.

Once the phone call was over, my parents and I looked at each other in stunned silence.

"Wow!" my mom said with a huge smile. "Look what you just did!" She gave me a tight hug and told me she was proud of me.

The first person I told the next day at school was Joanna and she said, "That's cool, I guess. I doubt it'll change anything though."

Oh Joanna, you smart, smug bundle of condescension. Everyone else was blown away. Every kid that signed that petition felt that they had challenged authority and won. The bell rang and when we walked into Monsieur G's classroom. He was standing by the blackboard, chalk in one hand, textbook in the other. No newspaper to be found. We learned about verb tenses that day. After the lesson, while we were practicing on work sheets, Monsieur G called Sam, Scott and Marcus to his desk. He spoke to them quietly and then shook each of their hands and ruffled Scott's hair.

That petition created change, not only in Monsieur G but in me as well. I learned that I had a voice and the right to use it. My feelings and opinions mattered. The experience gave me the confidence to keep standing up and speaking out when someone needed to be defended.

I don't repeat this story to suggest that I was a special person, or born for greatness, or anything like that. I'm sure most people, if not all people, have some experience in childhood that reveals to them their best self, a glimpse of their uniqueness and their potential. Those moments stick in our minds. They often inspire and encourage us. But we can also become distanced from them, lose track of them, and in strange ways, they can even turn against us.

From that moment on, I knew that I had a feisty streak in me. I had proven to myself that I could be strong and willful, ready to take on the world. I had no idea of the challenges that lay ahead or how my headstrong ways could also contribute to the downward spiral of my life. I could not imagine, back then, that some of my assertiveness and rebellious spirit could be misguided or misdirected. Nor did I expect that life would sometimes hit back at me, and *hard*, slowly turning the fearless little girl I used to be into the fragile woman I became.

* * *

When I was ten years old, I had a crush on Burt Reynolds. Burt was the rugged, mustachioed star of such gems as *Smokey and the Bandit* and *Deliverance*, but it was his performance in *Cannonball Run* that captured my pre-teen heart. While most of my friends decorated their bedroom walls with posters of heart-throbs like twenty-two-year-old Shaun Cassidy and sixteen-year-old Matt Dillon, I was swooning over forty-four-year-old Burt Reynolds.

Burt reminded me of my father. They shared the same dark, wavy hair and, of course, the mustache. My father lacked Burt's swagger but was handsome and something of a mystery to me. He and my mother were very different. She would disagree but I believe I inherited my feistiness from my mom, Shirley (she liked to say "Call me Sam, it's sexier"). My mom was the person to whom all of my friends confided things they couldn't discuss with their own parents. She was love personified and she kept her loving spirit even through a life of heartbreak and disappointment.

My father, on the other hand, was not affectionate. This was unfortunate but not surprising, given the people who raised him. Bubby and Zaida weren't the type of grandparents who gave big hugs, baked cookies, or knitted sweaters. They offered a firm but cool handshake and told us not to spill juice on their rugs.

While he was not father of the year, my dad and I had some good times. I loved how he would lie on his side on the couch and watch *Barney Miller* every night. He curled his legs in a way that formed a V-shaped space I could crawl into and watch with him. I appreciated when he waited in line with me to watch the early *Star Wars* movies. But my absolute favorite father/daughter activity was watching the Montreal Alouettes play football. I loved football and spend that time with my father.

A week after my tenth birthday, my parents told me they were getting a divorce. It was not a complete shock. My parents didn't fight a lot but there wasn't much laughter between them. Despite the fact that my mom was an affectionate woman, I never saw my parents hug or kiss. My mom told me, much later, that she knew on her honeymoon she was making a mistake and that their marriage was doomed. Both of my parents came from love deprived, unstable homes and saw each other as a way out. Marriage solved their immediate problems but that was the relationship had nowhere else to go.

My father immediately moved out of our home. When he left, everyone left behind – myself, my mother, my sister Lori, and my brother Billy – grew closer. Divorce doesn't have to be traumatic for children if both parents can put the needs of their children before themselves. My mother was able to do that. My father, however, had no interest in trying.

Divorce brought out the worst in him. His behavior was deplorable prior to the divorce but being single allowed him to show his true self. His time as a married father had held him back from the bachelor life he truly craved. Zaida had gifted him the family's thriving jewelry business in hopes that it would stay in the family for years to come. Instead, my father slowly ran it into the ground. He spent more time snorting cocaine and entertaining prostitutes in the stock room than he did working. Orders weren't filled or bills paid, although my father's popularity among his younger employees soared. He was the party dude who paid for the wine, women, and whatever else was wanted.

My mother did not ask him for alimony. She had never asked him for much, but she definitely needed child support once they were separated. She had been nineteen when they married, so she had little job experience and three kids to raise.

"I've got nothing to give her," my father would tell me when I begged him to help her out. "I've got no money left."

I felt guilty for asking and saw myself as a burden on him. I was also confused because he was living a lavish lifestyle. When I spent time with him, he'd show up at our house driving a cream-colored Corvette that screamed "Douchebag"! There were only two front seats, so I'd have to sit on the laps of the women who he brought with him.

I didn't bother to learn their names. It was never the same woman twice. My father had become a player. His new condo was attached to a health club that was popular among the recently divorced. Although I was only ten, I recognized its sleaziness. He had rigged the stereo to play Barry White as soon as he turned on the light switch.

My least favorite weekends were the ones I spent with my father and his girlfriend *du jour*. I sat by myself in front of the television, watching boring movies while my father and his lady friend were in the bedroom doing whatever she was probably paid to do. I stared at the front door and imagined myself running out, but I was too much of a good girl to go through with it.

The best weekends were the ones when Billy came with me. My big brother made everything better. My father rarely brought women around when Billy was with us. He probably thought I was too young to know what was going on, but Billy was fifteen and capable of reporting everything back to our mother.

Billy and I spent a lot of time playing made-up games while my father was out. Lava Island was my favorite. We pretended the floor was covered with lava and that the magazines we threw down were the only safe places to land. We leapt from magazine to magazine, and the first person to touch the boiling lava floor would lose. We were supposed to be bonding with my father during those weekends. Instead, we bonded with each other. Honestly, that was fine by me.

My older sister, Lori, never joined us. She had a different relationship with my father. She was seventeen and much more aware of his infidelity and recreational drug use. He hid these behaviors from me and didn't mention them to Billy. He actually bragged about them to Lori. He thought he was cool. But he wasn't. Not by a long shot. Nobody wants to find out that their father is a sleazebag, especially when you hear it straight from the sleazebag himself. I could understand my father wanting to impress Lori because Lori was a special young woman. She was as tough as she was beautiful. All of my friends were afraid of her. If she liked you, she'd go to war for you. If she didn't like you, watch out.

One Saturday morning, after a particularly bad incident with my father, I got home and ran straight to my bedroom without saying a word. Lori ran upstairs after me.

"What the hell happened?" she asked.

I explained waking up that morning to a loud knock at the door. I rubbed my ears and yelled for my father from my spot on his pullout couch. Out he came, wearing a tight paisley-patterned bathing suit. He was shirtless but wore two gold chains around his neck to complete the look.

I was still in my pajamas when he opened the door. Five of his friends walked in; I recognized Dwayne and Jeff, who were two of his young employees, but the three young women were strangers to me. My father was obviously expecting them but he hadn't warned me they were coming.

"We're going swimming," he said. "Get dressed and let's go!"

I reminded him that I hadn't brought a bathing suit. Apparently, that had been taken care of.

"I got you one!" said the perky blonde with dyed blue eyelashes. My father had asked her to buy me a swimsuit at the gift shop next to the pool in the condo.

I was stunned. I wasn't expecting company, especially for an 8 a.m. swim with these bargain basement Charlie's Angels. I put on the simple, blue bathing suit. It felt uncomfortable on so many levels, but I rejoined the gang. On our way out, my father grabbed a few beers. Even I knew that an insulin-dependent diabetic should not be drinking beer for breakfast, but I wasn't going to say anything.

Swimming was as unpleasant as expected. One of the brunettes was clearly there for Dwayne – she was all over him. The other brunette was Jeff 's date, and it was obvious that Blondie was there for my father. I just wanted to go home.

I got out of the pool and told my father I had a stomachache. I think he was actually relieved. It meant that he could spend less time with his nuisance of a daughter. I put my stuff in my bag, left the swimsuit on the bathroom floor, and asked him to drive me home.

I felt completely unloved and unwanted. I couldn't tell my mother what had happened because I knew she'd be upset. Every time my father broke my heart, hers broke twice as hard. I wasn't going to say a word to anyone, but Lori coaxed it out of me.

"What an asshole!" she yelled. "Don't worry, I'll handle it."

I may have been feisty, but Lori was fierce. She drove over to my father's place to confront him. When she got there, Dwayne said my father wasn't home. She knew he was lying and demanded to be let in. My father wasn't just an asshole, he was a weak asshole who was afraid of confrontation. He continued to pretend that he wasn't home, so she left.

I never stepped foot in his condo again.

Along with not paying alimony or child support, my father had stopped paying our phone bill, which we discovered when it was disconnected. Next, came my sister's car. My parents had bought it for her as a gift for her birthday and now he wanted it back. My mother begged him not to take it. My sister stored it at a friend's house until the situation was resolved. One night, my father asked my mom to meet him for dinner. She was excited, sure that he had changed his mind and was ready to contribute to our living expenses. She couldn't have been more wrong. As soon as she walked into the restaurant, he looked at her with a cocky grin and put three cassettes on the table. They were from Lori's car. He had tracked it down to her friend's house and taken it with his spare key. My mom was devastated.

It takes money to hire a lawyer to fight for child support, but this was money my mother didn't have. We went to court once. That morning, my father called our house and invited Billy, Lori, and me to meet him for breakfast. None of us knew what to expect. Once we were all seated, he looked at us and said, "Do you want to have a relationship with me?"

Since when is that a question a parent asks their kids? There was a brief pause before my sister answered, "No." I thought I should follow Lori's lead and answered the same.

Then it was Billy's turn. He said, "Yes." Lori and I both understood his answer. He wanted a dad, even this crappy one. Unfortunately for Billy, that wasn't the answer my father was hoping for. He was hoping for an escape. He wanted us to release him from his parental responsibilities so he could walk away guilt free.

Later that morning, the judge ordered him to pay a ridiculously low amount of child support, which he paid for one month before disappearing. He was free of his parental obligations, living in a different province. That was the last time we heard from him for several years.

Living in a broken home in 1980 was tough. I was the first kid in my elementary school to go through a divorce. My school wasn't prepared to deal with me. On Father's Day, our class project was to write poems and make cards for our dads. As soon as I heard the instructions, I asked if I could go to the bathroom, where I stayed crying for twenty minutes.

I returned to class and wrote a poem about my mom instead. It ended up being the perfect way to honor the parent that truly mattered. I never uttered the word "dad" again after that day in court.

We were better off without him. My mom worked hard to make ends meet and still be home for us after school. We moved from our big house to a much smaller townhouse, and we were happy. Billy took over as man of the house. I looked up to him in the way that I should have looked up to my father. We spent the next few years tackling things as a family, thinking the worst was behind us. I was angry with my father for abandoning me, but it brought me closer to the rest of my family, especially my older brother, Billy.

We didn't realize how quickly things could get worse.

CHAPTER TWO

After Billy

WEDNESDAY, MAY 27, 1987. It's amazing how much can change in just 24 hours.

I was still me on that Wednesday. I was still the outspoken seventeen-year-old who loved dancing and eating ice cream with her friends. Still the Marci who dreamed of becoming an actress and who had applied to a highly-respected theatre school to help make it happen. I was still feisty, fearless, and full of confidence.

The next day, Thursday, May 28, I was writing my final English exam before graduating from high school. I had barely started the afternoon portion of the test when the vice principal walked into the room. Mr. Sutherland was a serious looking fellow. Tall, mostly bald, glasses, and a black suit. Interruptions of any kind during an exam were rare, so the whole class looked up to see what was going on. Mr. Sutherland leaned over to whisper something into my teacher's ear. I saw my teacher turn his head in my direction and point right at me.

"Me? Was he here for me?" I asked myself.

He walked over to my desk, picked up my exam papers, and softly said, "Come with me, please."

I was confused but got up and followed him out of the room. On the way, I passed Mickey, one of my close friends, whose face was filled with concern. She mouthed, "Billy?"

"Don't worry," I mouthed back, with a reassuring smile. "He's okay."

Mickey knew that my big brother had been in the hospital for a few months, battling a liver disease that had taken far too long to diagnose. My mom had kept me out of school for a few days so I could be at the hospital with my family. As I was led out of my room, I realized that Mickey was probably right. This was about Billy. We had just been at the hospital last night – Billy had recently gone through his second liver transplant and hadn't been doing as well as the doctors had hoped, so we were all nervously waiting for his condition to improve.

I knew Billy's situation wasn't great, but I was frustrated at how negative my mother and her friends could be. My mom and her friends sat in the family waiting area, crying. I wanted them to stop because I felt that Billy was going to be fine. He was only twenty-one and had been healthy until recently. He was super athletic. He acted in school plays and played the drums. He was a total fucking rock star in my eyes. Since my father left, Billy had been my protector, my coach, my teacher, and my friend. He knew when to stand in front of me to protect me, and when to stand behind me, encouraging me to stand up for myself. He was going to be fine, and all these crying people were stressing me out.

As I walked down the long hallway to the main office, I kept expecting Mr. Sutherland to say something, but he said nothing. Nothing at all. He didn't even look in my direction. He seemed uncomfortable, which was making me feel uncomfortable. We passed the gym and I could hear the basketballs bouncing off the floor, which I found surprisingly calming. It reminded me of Sunday mornings in summertime, when I'd hear Billy wake up at six, grab his basketball and head out to the park to spend two hours shooting hoops before the rest of the neighborhood woke up. A few times, he'd surprised me by taking me with him. Those were my favorite days. Just me and Billy, chatting about life.

When we got to the main office, Mr. Sutherland opened the door for me and walked away. The school secretary instructed me to go into the principal's office. I wasn't a troublemaker, so being summoned to the principal's office was a new and unsettling experience for me. As soon as I walked in, I recognized the big man with the longish grey hair waiting for me. It wasn't the principal. It was my mom's friend, Isaac. My heart sank. My mother had sent her friend to take me out of school, in the middle of my final English exam. I felt sick to my stomach. Before Isaac could say a word, I asked "Is he . . .?"

I couldn't get myself to finish the question. With a pained face, Isaac nodded yes.

"He's dead? Billy's dead?" The words stung my tongue.

He told me to sit down but I just wanted to get to the hospital and see my brother before they took him away.

"I need to see him," I said firmly. "Take me to see him!"

I looked out the car window and cried just a little bit as we drove. I was in shock. He was my big brother. When I was eight, I was crowned Miss Grey Cup 1978 in a silly talent competition at summer camp; Billy was older and cooler, but he immediately rushed on stage to lift me up on his shoulders and carry me around with pride. He was my protector and he was always on my side. How could that loving, sweet, heroic big brother really be dead?

My teenaged brain couldn't wrap itself around the thought of this gorgeous, loving boy being dead so young. Maybe my mother had been trying to protect me by not telling me how serious things were. Maybe she was also protecting herself. She explained to me a few weeks later that having me skip an exam would have meant admitting to herself that Billy was dying, and she was just not prepared to do that. In a weird way, she felt that sending me to school would keep Billy alive. I understood, but it just made the reality of the situation all the more devastating.

"We're only 10 minutes away, you okay?" Isaac asked.

I barely nodded yes, but thought, "No! I'm not! I will never be okay again!"

Was it my fault? I suddenly wondered if I should I have noticed sooner that Billy was sick.

I started thinking about all the signs I might have missed. I wished his illness had come with flashing lights and a siren. But who had heard of Wilson's Disease? I hadn't. As it turned out, Wilson's Disease is a genetic disorder in which copper builds up in the body. Billy was born with it. We had no idea. A person with Wilson's can't process copper and when copper accumulates, they become ill. Billy didn't have most of the usual symptoms, making him difficult to diagnose. As I remember it, he started feeling sick in his late teens. He was getting tired easily. He was also jaundiced. These were signs of liver trouble but that's all we knew.

If it had been caught sooner, the disease would have been treatable. Instead, this seemingly healthy boy got sicker and sicker with every misdiagnosis thrown at him. First the doctors thought he had mono, then hepatitis. When a liver biopsy finally gave us the answer we were searching for, the disease had progressed too far and he needed a liver transplant. When that transplant failed, he was given a second.

Even with all of this happening, I didn't realize how serious things were. It was Billy. *My* Billy. He was the invisible armor I wore every day to make me feel safe. When he was ten and I was five and in bed with the chicken pox, he wrote me letters from summer camp to let me know I could sleep with all of his stuffed animals. When I was ten and he was fifteen and we were at camp together, he never made me feel like an annoying little sister, even when I would visit his cabin for big brother hugs and reassurance. When I turned fifteen and started to feel the pressure to lose weight, I asked him if I needed to be skinnier to be prettier. He looked me straight in the eyes and said, "You are not only beautiful exactly as you are, but you are also one of the smartest and strongest people I know." When he was 21, lying in the hospital, too weak to lift his fork to feed himself and having to let his sister do it for him, he turned to her and said, "If it had to be any of us, I'm so glad it was me." That was Billy. The protector. I never thought for a second that he wasn't going to be okay.

"Are you ready?" Isaac asked as we walked into the hospital. He meant well but what a stupid question. Was I ready? For what? To see my dead brother? No, I was absolutely not ready. But I just nodded and kept walking.

I was taken into the intensive care unit and saw Billy lying in his bed. All of the machines he had been connected to were silent. His eyes were closed, his cheeks were still swollen, his skin was still jaundiced, but he was ever so handsome to me. My sister was standing next to him. It was her birthday. How shitty is that? I took his hand and held it between both of mine. It felt cold.

I don't know how to explain this, but he didn't seem dead to me. Never having seen a dead body before, I had nothing to compare this to "Are they sure?" I whispered to my sister. She looked at me confused. Of course they were sure.

But none of it seemed real. I held his hand as long as they let me. After what didn't feel like nearly long enough, I was led away and into a room in the back of the intensive care unit reserved for grieving families. Leaving him was the hardest thing I ever had to do. I walked past a few of Billy's favorite nurses and could see them crying, especially the small brunette that Billy said had a crush on him. One morning when I walked in, just as she was leaving his room, he motioned for me to come closer, and whispered with a coy smile, "She wants me." We laughed. I think he was right.

When I got to the family grieving room, I saw my mom, Eddie (her live-in boyfriend), and Billy's girlfriend. Everyone was sobbing. I was too mad to cry. Mad at the world. Mad at the doctors. Mad at God. Mad at myself. I should have been a better sister.

I have no memory of leaving the hospital or even who drove me home. I do, however, remember sitting in someone's car and hearing, "I Would Die 4 U" by Prince on the radio and bursting into tears. Billy was the biggest Prince fan. He and I must have watched *Purple Rain* ten times together. I cried, but hearing Prince at that moment felt like I had been given an extra two minutes and fifty-four seconds with my big brother. A few days later, we would bury him with the *Sign o' the Times* record that he had listened to in the hospital.

Half an hour after we got home, I was feeling tipsy from the screwdrivers that Isaac had poured me. At seventeen, I wasn't of legal drinking age, but nobody knew what to say or do with me in the situation and vodka seemed an easy distraction. In fairness, I didn't know what to do with myself either. I went into Billy's bedroom and saw my sister sitting on his bed.

"I guess we have to like each other now", she said.

Lori and I were different and often had trouble connecting. We sat on his bed for close to a minute before she walked out. I lay there for another fifteen, realizing with a new terror how vulnerable I was. If this could happen to Billy, horrible things could happen to anybody. I'm pretty sure that the moment before this realization was the very last moment that I ever felt safe. "Marci, pick up the phone!" I heard my mom yell up the stairs.

The phone had started ringing the moment we got home as people who had heard the news called with their condolences. But this call was different. I picked up the phone. The voice on the other end belonged to someone at the admissions office of the theatre school. Billy had helped me choose and rehearse my audition monologue. It was from the Arthur Miller play *All My Sons*. He had performed it in high school a few years earlier. The call was to let me know that I had been accepted into the program. Talk about a bittersweet moment. I thanked her, looked up and thought, "Thank you, Billy."

Immediately after I hung up, the phone rang again. I was closest to it so I answered. I could not have been less prepared for the excited little voice I heard on the other end. My brother had worked as a counsellor at a summer camp the year before, and the person calling had been one of his campers. He said Billy was his favorite counsellor and he was calling to say "Hi." How the hell was I going to handle this? Tell an eight-year-old kid that his favorite counsellor had just passed away? I asked to speak to his mom. When she answered, I said, "Billy died today." I apologized for having to share the news with her. The thought of her having to turn to her son and tell him what happened hurt my heart. I hung up the phone and almost immediately the guilt sunk in.

"It should have been me," I thought.

Billy meant so much to so many people. The world still needed him. Those five words became my mantra. The message I would hear in my head every day from the day Billy left me. "It should have been me."

At that moment, I decided if I was going to be stealing his place in this lifetime, I had to earn it. I had to earn my place on this planet, and I couldn't do that by being ordinary. I had to be *spectacular*.

The problem was that I wasn't spectacular. Not even close. I wasn't funny enough, or smart enough, or interesting enough to be worthy of my existence. The one thing I thought I could possibly control was how I looked. If I couldn't *be* good enough, I could try to *look* pretty, and maybe that would do. To my teenaged brain, being pretty enough meant being skinny enough.

It would take me a long time to learn there would never be such a thing as 'skinny enough,' at least, not for me.

Billy's death gave birth to my eating disorder. Being skinny was how I would project myself to the world and protect myself. My eating disorder would fill the gap left by Billy. But where Billy had been kind, warm, and loving, my disorder was cruel, judgmental, and deceptive. At first, it seemed like the perfect distraction. It was easier to focus on my empty stomach than his empty room. Physical pain I could handle. At barely seventeen, I was not emotionally equipped for life without Billy.

CHAPTER THREE

The Shape of Rebellion

HOW DOES A TEENAGE GIRL, who doesn't do drugs (too scary) or drink alcohol (too fattening) rebel against God and the world for taking her brother? I did it by losing my virginity in a boating shack.

Billy had been dead a month. Billy was a good guy. I was a good girl. So why were bad things happening to us? I began to think the answer was to stop being so good. Most kids believed that they were invincible at my age, but knew the opposite was true. I felt vulnerable and powerless, and I hated it. I tried to use dieting and weight loss to regain a sense of control over my life, but it didn't feel extreme enough. I needed something bigger. I needed to have sex.

My original plan for that summer was to teach dance at the same overnight camp where Billy had planned to work. With him gone, I wasn't sure I wanted to go. My brain felt foggy. I looked fine and acted fine, but I was the farthest thing from fine. My brother was gone and I felt like a lost kitten trying to be a tiger. His co-workers nevertheless convinced me to attend.

Virginity is a weird thing. We're taught to think of it as a precious gift to cherish and protect until we're ready to hand it over to the right person. Wise people say that the decision to lose our "innocence" should be made after serious thought and reflection. I never felt that way about it, though. When I was twelve years old, my friend Joanna shared her virginity plans with me over a bowl of chocolate chip ice cream. To Joanna, waiting to have sex until you were in love didn't make sense.

"My lack of experience will mean that I'm going to suck the first time I do it. I'd rather pick someone random the first time so I can be good for the person I really care about," she explained.

She was so damn smart. I couldn't argue with that kind of logic.

Until that summer, I hadn't been sexually active. I'd engaged in some making out, a little over the clothes groping and dry humping, but nothing close to intercourse. I was ready to change that. Somewhere, in the back of my brain, I felt that having sex would prove I was desirable and at the same time make me tough. If I was going to raise my confidence and self-esteem, I needed to feel desirable and tough.

The owner of the camp held a staff meeting on our first night to introduce himself to us and for us to introduce ourselves to each other. It was a great way for me to scout prospective deflowerers. As the meeting went on, I started to feel a little more at ease about working there without Billy. Everyone was welcoming, and I was excited to spend the next eight weeks teaching dance. When it was time to head back to our cabins, a boy named Matthew approached me and offered to walk with me. He told me he had noticed me earlier in the day and was interested in getting to know me. I said sure.

During our walk, I found out that Matthew went to school with a few kids I knew in the city. He had an older sister and loved playing hockey. Matthew was cute and he was nice. Too nice. I wasn't looking for a summer romance to write about in my diary or giggle about with my girlfriends. I wanted to get laid. When we got to my cabin, he kissed my cheek before walking away. We didn't talk much again after that night.

A couple of weeks into the summer, I realized I was enjoying myself. I got along well with the girls I worked with and dancing all day gave me a sense of peace over my life and my body. Even though Billy's death still weighed heavily on my heart, dancing helped me to cope. It also helped me to appreciate my body. It didn't cure my eating disorder but I found myself less preoccupied with food and calories. I felt healthier. I was nevertheless as determined as ever to follow through on my plan.

Suddenly, as I left the dining hall one night, I thought I had found The One. Sean was the strong, silent type. I'd seen him around camp and thought he was great to look at, but I had never heard him speak. He had blonde hair that swooped in the front in a very eighties style. He had an earring in his left ear. There was a George Michael, "Wake Me Up Before You Go-Go" quality to him that I found attractive.

"You're Marci, right?" he asked as I walked past.

"Yup," I answered.

Then, through a big, beautiful smile he said, "I knew Billy. He was a really good guy. I think it's great that you're working here this summer."

My heart melted a little and I thought, "Maybe the sex wouldn't have to be completely meaningless."

I started walking towards him to continue our conversation. As I approached him, a mop of brown, curly hair, attached to a burly teenaged girl jumped in front of me and into his arms. He had a girlfriend, and she looked like she was ready to beat the crap out of me. She also looked like she was used to girls hitting on her boyfriend and she was not interested in sharing him.

"Abort mission!" my brain warned.

It was not meant to be. For the next two weeks, I continued to get into the camp spirit and make some friends. My favorite nights were spent at the little poutine shack down the road. After the campers were in bed, some of the staff would head there to hang out. There was a jukebox loaded with the hits that my dance instructor friends played. It was there that I caught Lance checking me out. He was the head of boating and canoeing.

"Who's that guy?" I asked my friend Amy through bites of poutine.

"That's Lance. Nice guy, but I wouldn't date him," she warned. "He's just out for sex."

"Perfect!" I thought.

I strolled over to him and said hello.

"Hey," he said back.

"I'm Marci," I said.

"Ok," he said. "You're cute."

"Thanks."

"Cool," he responded.

I could feel myself getting dumber the longer I stood there.

"Wanna walk?" he asked.

"Sure."

We walked down the road discussing the Iran-Contra Affair. Just kidding. I think he was telling me about his dream car. I threw in a few nods and some "uh huhs" to make it seem like I was listening. In reality, I was trying to figure out how to ask for what I wanted.

As it turns out, if you want to have sex with a guy, all you have to do is ask. I can't remember how the conversation went exactly, but I told him that I knew about his reputation. He tried to deny it, but I told him not to bother: I was hoping that it was true. I made it clear that I was interested in getting to know him better, or at least getting naked. He was surprised by my candor. "Are you sure?" he asked me. I said that I was. He grabbed a stick from the ground and drew a line in the dirt between the two of us.

"If you want to have sex with me, step over the line," he instructed. "If you don't, then stay where you are. I'll give you ten seconds to decide."

Kudos to him for confirming my consent. He was well ahead of his time for that consideration. I hesitated a few seconds so that I wouldn't seem desperate, and then took a step forward.

"Cool," he said.

After a little more flirting and a fair bit of sexual innuendo (most of which went over his head), we agreed to get together over the next few days to seal the deal. Looking back, I probably should have told him that our hook-up was going to be my first. I didn't. I was worried that he wouldn't want to have sex with a virgin so I kept this tidbit to myself. A couple of days later, Lance walked over to me during breakfast and handed me a note as he passed by. The note read: "Meet me at the boating shack at 1 a.m."

"Holy crap!" I screamed in my head, "Mission 'Get Marci Laid' is a go!"

My heart started racing. I felt excited and also nauseous. This *was* a big deal. Once it was done, there was no way to undo it. There were no virginity do-overs. But I was a girl on a mission, with no intention of changing my mind. I didn't tell anyone except for Amy. She had been friends with Lance for years and thought I was making a mistake, but she was still supportive.

"Make sure he uses a condom," she said. "Oh, and tell me everything in the morning."

* * *

Having sex for the first time can be daunting, but having sex for the first time at a children's summer camp brings daunting to a new level. Sex on camp property was forbidden. I knew that, but it wasn't going to stop me. Until that point, I had been a rule follower. I'd never gotten into any major trouble in school. I'd never stolen anything from anybody. The closest I came to shoplifting was when I was thirteen and saw my friend Stacy slide the book "How to Kiss with Confidence" into her backpack while we were in a bookstore at the Cavendish mall. I had nothing to do with it and she was never caught, but I still spent months worrying that I was going to get arrested for it. I had always tried to do the right thing and here I was preparing to do something very wrong.

After Lance handed me his note, the rest of the day flew by. Before I knew it, it was time for the campers to go to bed. Two hours later, all staff had to be in their cabins for the night. While everyone's night was winding down, mine was about to start. I slept in a cabin with two counsellors and twelve kids. I had to wait until all of them were asleep before I snuck out. I didn't trust the counsellors enough to fill them in on my plans, so I had to be very careful not to wake anyone. I waited an extra twenty minutes until everyone was asleep before starting my ninja-like escape. Each of the cabins was old and built of wood. It was challenging to sneak out without loud creaking sounds. I held my breath as I tiptoed through the cabin and out the door.

My next challenge was to get past the other cabins in my unit without being spotted. Walking in front of them felt too risky, so I crawled behind them through the high grass and prickly bushes. When I stood up, I shook off the dirt and prepared myself for the sprint ahead. I had to cross an open field to get to where I was going. At least two members of the head staff patrolled the area in jeeps every night. They were on the lookout for any-one who didn't belong there, including wayward staff up to no good. Not knowing when they'd be back, I ran as fast as I could and hoped for the best. I finally reached the canoe shack, sweaty and nervous.

I knocked on the door and when Lance opened it, I noticed a mattress on the floor, a lit candle in the corner, and a small radio playing a string of eighties ballads. I was worried about the candle in a wooden cabin, but I appreciated his effort. I also realized that I was probably not the first girl to visit his love shack.

"So, how are you?" he asked me.

"Let's just do it," I said.

While I appreciated his romantic gestures, I really just wanted to get the deed done and get back to my cabin.

I was familiar with the cliché that a girl always remembers her first but, to be honest, I barely do. I have memory flashes of us kissing and him pushing my head to his crotch, which must have been disappointing for him, as I had never done that before. Then he climbed on top of me. About twenty seconds before penetration, I whispered, "This is my first time."

"What?" he asked. He didn't expect that news. I reassured him that it was what I wanted and told him to continue. The whole thing was over pretty quickly. I remember there was less pain and blood than I had anticipated. It was fine. Most importantly, it was done. Mission complete.

I put my clothes on and Lance and I exchanged an awkward hug before I left. I felt a little emotionally numb and looked forward to talking to Amy about it in the morning. But right now, it was close to 2 a.m., well past curfew, and my main concern was getting back to my cabin without being caught by the head staff. I failed at that.

Two head staffers, Craig and Bryan, tracked me down with huge grins on their faces, enjoying the fact that they had the power to get me thrown out of camp. They let me pass after some creepy teasing. I got back to my cabin, crawled into bed, and stared at the ceiling for the rest of the night.

If I was a character in a Nicholas Sparks novel, Lance would have defended my honor against Craig and Bryan, and then spent the summer proving to me that our sexcapade, which started as a simple act of teenage rebellion, would end as a true and lasting love.

But it wasn't a Nicholas Spark novel, it was my life. Lance was friendly to me for a week before I found out that he was having sex with the arts and crafts instructor. I'd love to say that it didn't bother me, but that would be a lie. I didn't care about Lance, but it made me feel disposable.

Of course, this wasn't fair to Lance. He had behaved exactly as I'd asked him to. I'd wanted a transactional relationship and I'd got one. That he'd moved on and I was hurt was my problem. As much as I tried to act like a bad girl, it just wasn't me. Not at this point in my life. I had a difficult time admitting that to myself, though, and it would not be the last time that the consequences of my willful tendencies, my rebelliousness, and my sexual adventuring left me confused and alone in a place that was darker and more disturbing than where I wanted to be.

I did manage to enjoy the rest of the summer, teaching and hanging out with my friends, but I looked forward to getting back home and to starting theatre school in the fall. While I wasn't feeling as strong or empowered as I would have wished, I did feel a little more hopeful than when the summer started. I was more comfortable with my body and I thought maybe I was going to be okay. Unfortunately, life had other plans.

CHAPTER FOUR

My New Skill

I T HAD BEEN A MONTH since I'd been back from camp and four months since my brother died. Theatre school had just started and, at my mother's insistence, I had made an appointment with my doctor for a physical exam. Not surprisingly, my mom had become extra vigilant about my health after Billy died.

On the day of my physical, I felt good despite an irritating head cold. Between dance classes and playing sports with my friends, I had always been an active kid without any health issues. Teaching dance that summer had helped me reconnect with my body and stop obsessing over every calorie I consumed. I had enough self-awareness, even at that age, to recognize that I had been developing an unhealthy preoccupation with my weight right after losing Billy, and I was trying hard to nip it in the bud.

My doctor, who I'll call Dr. Clueless, had also been Billy's doctor, so he was well aware of the loss I had experienced. Dr. C walked into the examining room, said hello and instructed me to hop on the scale to be weighed. Despite the progress I'd been making with my body image issues, I did not want to be weighed. After having sex with the boating dude, I'd started taking birth control pills, which resulted in a slight weight gain. A few pounds from the pill is very common, and I knew I shouldn't be overly stressed about it because it was only five pounds and I was still well within a healthy weight range.

But my feelings about my body weren't always rational and the idea of hearing exactly how much I weighed terrified me. I wanted to eat well, stay active, and let my body settle exactly where it was supposed to. That would be challenging if I heard a number that upset me. I shared this information with Dr. C.

"Seeing my weight could really mess me up," I explained. He told me I was being ridiculous and that being weighed was an essential part of a routine physical exam.

"Stop acting like a baby," he teased.

Reluctantly, I did as I was told. I stood on the scale, wearing only a pair of underwear and one of those flimsy robes that barely covered my butt. I didn't want to be standing there. I had made that fact perfectly clear. I took a deep breath then exhaled as much air as I could, trying to make myself as light as possible, while I closed my eyes tight.

"Please don't tell me what I weigh," I begged.

I was anxious and vulnerable and completely unprepared for what came next. Dr. C berated me with insult after insult about how fat I'd become. With a look of disgust on his face, he pointed at my stomach and said, "Look at that! What is that?" He told me that while I wasn't medically overweight, society was skinny and if I wanted to fit into society, I had to lose ten pounds. He didn't stop there.

"If I were you," he warned, "I wouldn't be caught dead wearing a bathing suit!"

I was stunned. Nobody had ever commented negatively on my weight before and I had always been one of the skinnier girls in my peer group. It was confusing. Logically, I knew that I wasn't overweight, but if my doctor was calling me fat and unattractive, maybe he was right.

I could hear sounds of disapproval coming from the adjoining room where my mother was waiting. She wanted to run into the room and tell this idiot to leave her baby alone, but she was afraid I'd be angry with her for running to my rescue. So, she just listened, feeling helpless and guilty.

Ever since I was little, my mom had referred to me as her "best eater." I've always loved food and had a voracious appetite. After holiday brunches, when Lori and Billy unbuckled their pants in uncomfortable fullness, I asked what was for dinner. I'd try any food, any time, and was encouraged by my parents to do so. I was fortunate to have good genes, a quick metabolism, and an active lifestyle, all of which made my weight a non-issue until that day at my doctor's office.

"You'd be perfect," he continued, "if you just lost a little weight."

For fuck's sake. He was telling me to diet. I had spent the last two months trying not to worry about food and calories and now my doctor, a medical professional, didn't simply suggest that I lose weight, he was *instructing* me to. I was shocked.

After my physical exam was completed, I sat in his office while he informed me of his plan to make me more physically acceptable. I had to keep a daily journal of the foods I ate and portion sizes. At the end of every week, he wanted me to return to his office where he would analyze and scrutinize the items on my list. He wanted me to do this until I lost the weight that he deemed necessary.

I left his office determined not to let his plan screw me up. I promised myself that I would not go back to under-eating and obsessing about my diet. My intentions were good but, sadly, unrealistic. At lunch with my mom that afternoon, I ordered a piece of dry toast and a cup of black tea. Eating anything more than that would have felt gluttonous.

The full impact of Dr. C's words wasn't immediate. For the first week, I still allowed myself to eat most of the foods I enjoyed. My stepfather, Eddie, was a caterer and I loved when he took me shopping with him for food. We'd go into places that offered samples and, at this point, I still enjoyed trying new and exciting foods, although in smaller portions. I also enjoyed the occasional nutritionally deficient but delicious snack food. At the end of that first week, I brought my journal to Dr. C's office, handed it to him, and got the tongue lashing of my life.

"A Pop Tart?" he screamed at me. "You ate a Pop Tart? Are you crazy, Marci? You're basically just eating two pieces of cake with icing in between!"

I felt shamed, which was his intention.

"Do you want to stay chubby?" Dr. C asked rhetorically.

My brain knew that he was wrong. I wasn't chubby. I stood 5'6 inches tall and weighed 130 pounds. I was fit and I was healthy. And what if I was chubby? Why would that even matter? Why was he so concerned about how I looked in a bathing suit? Why did he want me to care so much about that?

He was out of line and far outside his duties as a medical doctor. The logical side of my brain understood that, but it wasn't the logical side that spoke the loudest to me. The seeds of my eating disorder had been planted when Billy died, and I had been trying hard not to cultivate them. Now, thanks to Dr. Clueless, they were watered and given all the sunlight they needed.

This time, when I left his office, it was with only one intention. I was going to get skinny. The first thing I did was make a list of all of the foods I could no longer eat. At the top of the list: Pop Tarts. I also stopped eating fried foods, butter, margarine, and mayonnaise. I limited my bread and cheese consumption and gave up high fat foods like salmon and eggs, even though they were healthy. I had no idea what a proper portion size was, so I asked a friend's mom if I could borrow her Weight Watchers manual as a guideline. One morning, a year earlier, when I was visiting Billy in the hospital, I told him I was thinking about joining Weight Watchers. I remember him shaking his head in total disagreement and saying, "They'll never accept you. You're perfect as you are."

Sorry, Billy.

Once I got the manual, I started following their portion suggestions but quickly theorized that if I cut these portion sizes in half, I could lose weight even quicker. Attending theatre school was conducive to my weight loss goals because of the long hours involved. I was at school for close to twelve hours a day, and my mother was unaware that I didn't eat all day. On weekends I had to be more resourceful. I ate my meals alone, in my room. The small food scale I had purchased kept my protein intake exactly where I decided it should be, one quarter of what Weight Watchers suggested. I started to lose weight and I loved it.

My classmate, Rachel Schwartz, inspired the next change to my diet. Rachel was a vegetarian and she challenged me to give up red meat and chicken for a week. I enjoyed beef and chicken but soon discovered that I enjoyed losing weight even more. I saw Rachel's challenge as an excuse to add more foods to my do-not-eat list. That was the day I became a vegetarian. It wasn't for moral or ethical reasons. It was because, in some twisted way, I liked depriving myself of the foods I enjoyed so that I could reach my weight loss goal.

My cravings didn't go away immediately, but I found a way to satisfy them without negatively impacting the number on my bathroom scale. Whenever I would get hungry and interesting food ideas popped into my head, I prepared them and gave them to Lori to eat. She was a great sport at first. She ate every bizarre concoction I came up with, from onion-flavored cream cheese sandwiched between two shortbread cookies, to nacho chips covered in peanut butter and rice crispy cereal. This went on for a few weeks until she figured out that I was feeding her to avoid feeding myself, and then she refused to play along.

Lori had a hard time watching the changes to my body. One day, while I was stepping out of the shower, Lori walked into the bathroom and screamed; she was horrified by the sight of my spinal bones sticking sharply out of my back. She begged me to start eating more. I felt horrible that I had upset her, but her reaction also thrilled me because it validated that I was on the right track.

Lori was also disturbed by my meal preparation. My mother used to buy cans of tiny mandarin segments packed in juice. I loved them. In an attempt to remove the sugar from the juice, I rinsed each mandarin slice individually. My sister watched me do this once and, after that, avoided being in the kitchen with me.

My body felt weaker. I got tired more easily. But seeing bones where I used to see a thicker layer of skin was exciting. Watching my collar bone and hip bones become more and more pronounced filled me with pride. I wore every worried comment and expression of concern from friends and family as badges of honor. When I bumped into an old high school friend who gasped and said, "What happened? You're shrinking!" I felt elated. It reached the point where the reflection I saw of myself in the mirror was completely distorted. Despite being able to feel my bones protruding through my skin, I still saw layers of fat that needed to be removed.

On a trip to the mall one afternoon, I bumped into my sister who said, "You look good."

You look good. That was all she said, but that one comment sent me spiraling with anxiety. I was so used to her telling me that I was too skinny, that to my skewed, disordered brain, she was telling me that I had actually gained weight. I burst into tears, left the mall, and eliminated a few more foods from my ever-shrinking diet.

Losing weight had taken over most of my thoughts, leaving room for little else. I was in my first year of a three-year theatre program and was struggling to keep up. There was so much that I loved about the program, but as my body shrunk, so did my confidence. In the past, I'd always been eager to show off my dancing skills. Now, I was too caught up in thinking about the numbers I produced on my bathroom scale.

On my last visit to Dr. Clueless, he said, "You look like you've lost a lot of weight, hop on the scale and let's see where you're at." I watched as he kept moving the small, sliding weight more and more to the left, balancing out at 102 pounds. "That's practically 25 pounds! That's a lot of weight. Don't lose anymore!"

"Oh yeah?" I thought, my rebelliousness roaring back. "Just watch me!"

I stopped seeing Dr. Clueless after that day because I had proven to him that I wasn't the chubby girl he had berated in his office. I no longer had any use for him, and I'd lost all respect for him as a physician. I wish I could say that was enough for me. I wish I could say that the feisty girl who used to stand up for herself was able to do again, reclaiming her body and her health. But that wouldn't be the truth.

I had lost the first ten pounds to please him, and the next fifteen as a "fuck you" for his making me feel bad about myself. What I didn't realize, of course, was that I was the one getting screwed. My eating disorder was taking over my life. I started to believe that losing weight was my best skill and that being skinny was a more reasonable goal than being an actress.

I was making some great friends at school and I enjoyed a lot of the classes. But obsessing over food and my body had become my coping mechanism when things got challenging in my life and things were about to get challenging once again.

CHAPTER FIVE

Double Lives

"ALWAYS REMEMBER TO BE POLITE," my stepfather would advise me repeatedly. "Being polite is crucial when interacting with people." This was sound advice but a little odd coming from him.

My mom met Eddie through one of her oldest friends, Sarah. Eddie was originally from Montreal but had been living in the United States for the last few years. When Sarah heard he was moving back to Montreal, she decided that he and mom should meet. Lori, Billy, and I joined my mom for dinner one evening at Sarah's place, where Eddie was the guest of honor. It turned out the two of them had worked together when they were teenagers. This meant that she was felt a little less nervous about getting set-up – he wasn't exactly a stranger.

This was important, because the whole concept of dating again made my mom a bit uneasy. After her relationship with my father, it wasn't easy for her to trust somebody else, and she refused to stay with another dishonest man. In recent years, she mostly focused on providing a safe and loving home for my siblings and me. Eddie was someone who could potentially break through my mom's distrust; she remembered him fondly and they had been reunited by one of her closest friends, so what could go wrong?

Eddie was a big man. He stood over six feet tall and was quite broad, with a gregarious personality. Everybody liked Eddie. Everybody except my sister. There was something about him that made Lori uneasy, although she couldn't specify it. We thought she was being overly protective of my mom.

All throughout that dinner party, Eddie kept us entertained with stories of his life in the U.S. and some of the more interesting parties he had catered. Cooking was something he was very passionate about, and his passion was contagious. After the party, Eddie and my mom started dating.

While my sister refused to give him a chance, Billy and I grew close to Eddie. He went out of his way to do nice things for us and I was comforted by how attentive he was to my mom from the beginning of their relationship. I wanted her to have someone in her life who truly loved her and treated her the way she deserved to be treated.

After a few months of steady dating, Eddie moved into our home. Oftentimes, a man will put a lot of time and energy into wooing the woman he's interested in, only to have it wane once they become settled in the relationship. Eddie was not one of those men. On Valentine's Day, he decorated their bedroom with heart-shaped cut outs and pink and red balloons. On my mother's birthday, he filled the room with flowers. I was happy that she was happy.

I had my own special relationship with Eddie. He loved talking about food and I loved hearing about it. I would listen intently as he described in detail every dish he served at his events. Cornish hens were his favorite. Sometimes he served them with roasted vegetables and risotto or caramelized carrots. I loved our trips to the markets where Eddie bought his produce and fish. We spent hours walking through these markets, brainstorming ideas for the next bar mitzvah or charity gala. My diet, at this point, included just a few solid foods, mainly fruits and vegetables. It was hard to resist sampling the goodies at the market, but I managed. Eddie wasn't thrilled about my diet and always tried to tempt me with french fries and milkshakes on our drives home. I politely declined.

Eddie had a certain charm that put people at ease. My friends, most of whom had never met my father, were very comfortable around Eddie. He'd even managed to get my father's parents to like him. My grandparents didn't like me, but they liked Eddie after meeting him just a few times.

They liked him so much that when my grandfather died, Eddie was asked to be a pallbearer.

In spite of his attributes, Eddie had a few quirks. For one thing, he drove slowly. Painfully slowly. I'm all for being a cautious driver, but he took slow and steady to another level. Whenever Eddy drove us anywhere, we always added extra time to our expected arrival. We also never knew what car he would be driving from week to week. Instead of buying or leasing a car, Eddie rented them and changed them often. "Why settle for one car, when you can have them all?" he'd say. It was a little weird but no cause for concern.

What was concerning was his temper. I only witnessed it once, before Billy died, but it was enough to make me view Eddie differently. It happened when he was preparing a lobster dinner for my family. I'd never eaten fresh lobster before and had agreed to try some it along with the big salad that I had prepared for myself. When we were all seated at the kitchen table, he brought each of us our own lobsters to eat. Lori, Billy, and my mom started cracking them open and pulling out the juicy meat inside. I was instantly put off by the green gook at the center of my lobster's spine.

"What's that?" I asked Eddie as he placed it in front of me.

"Don't worry about it, it's nothing," he answered

"It looks gross!" I continued.

Without warning, Eddie turned on me and yelled in his booming voice, "Stop acting like a spoiled brat and eat your dinner!"

I froze.

"You're not a baby, so stop acting like one," he continued.

Before he could say another word, my mother got out of her seat, walked around the back of my chair, put her hands on my shoulders, and said to Eddie, quietly but firmly: "Don't you ever speak to one of my children that way again."

He told her that I was being unreasonable and threatened to walk out the door if she didn't discipline me.

"I'd like you to leave," she told him. "Right now."

He did leave. When he came back a few hours later, he was in a much calmer state with apologies for everyone. I told him that I forgave him, but

I never felt quite as safe around him after that. This incident reinforced to me how protective my mother was of her children.

Around this time, Billy was starting to show signs of his liver disease, but we still had no idea what was happening to him. When he was admitted to hospital, my family visited him every day. Billy and Eddie continued their close relationship in the hospital and played basketball with a toy ball and net Eddie had set up in front of his bed. There was a large plant in the corner of the room that one of Eddie's clients had bought to cheer up Billy. I was happy that the two of them had bonded and that Billy could have a strong male figure around him.

When Billy died a few months later, my father was living five hours away in Toronto. Every few weeks, he and I would have a superficial phone conversation. It felt strained and awkward. Eddie would now be the only consistent male figure in my life. My mother engraved Eddie's name on Billy's tombstone as a way of honoring their special friendship. She married Eddie soon after.

Life never went back to normal after Billy was gone, but we tried to create a "new normal." My sister worked as a dental assistant, I was in theatre school, and my mom and Eddie settled into married life. Eddie's schedule was challenging at times. Every second weekend, he was in charge of catering a large church brunch. There was so much involved in this event that he needed to wake up in the middle of the night to prepare for it. He told me about all the details of his drive to the industrial kitchen he rented, the preparation, the cooking and serving, and the clean-up afterwards. He was gone all day and into the evening.

These bi-weekly events annoyed Lori and me because Eddie got uptight the night before and stressed us all out. Despite having regularly worked this event for close to two years, he was always anxious the night before. He paced back and forth in the living room, deep in thought. We couldn't speak to him or bother him while he was processing what needed to be done the next day. We also had to be very quiet.

"Eddie needs a good night sleep so he can wake up early tomorrow!" my mother would yell downstairs to us when we were watching TV or listening to music.

And then there were the socks. Eddie had a pair of "lucky socks" that he made sure were washed and ready to wear before every brunch. It was a ritual he would not mess with. I couldn't imagine what kind of brunch disaster he hoped to avoid with these lucky socks, but they were a crucial part of his preparation.

Just nine months after Billy died and six months after officially becoming my stepdad, the secret Eddie had been keeping from us all finally came out. After a late night at school, I walked into my house and found my mother and sister at the kitchen table waiting for me.

"Sit down, I have some news to tell you about Eddie," my mom said, her voice trembling.

As far as I knew, Eddie had left early that day for one of his brunches. My first thought was that he had gotten into a car accident. Driving too slowly.

"What happened? Is he okay?" I asked.

"He's fine, but he's been arrested," she continued.

I heard the words she was saying, but they weren't making sense.

"He has been lying to us from the second we met him. He's not a caterer. He's a bank robber."

My head started spinning. I had a million questions running through my mind, but could only utter one: "What?"

Eddie had been wanted by the police for two years in connection with forty-seven bank robberies he had committed between Montreal and Toronto. They had given him the nickname 'The Satchel Bandit' or 'Satch' for short, because of the satchel he carried with him during his heists. For two years, he had managed to elude the police. On this day, however, he wasn't so lucky.

Eddie had left a bank with $1,600 of its money when he was chased by a limo driver parked outside. He hadn't put up much of a fight and was forthcoming with the police after he was caught.

The police let us know that the gun Eddie used was just a toy and that the tellers described him as "polite." Of course, they did. Eddie always preached the importance of being polite. Personally, I would question how courteous it is to point a gun, even a fake one, in someone's face as you instruct them to hand over the money.

I had no idea what to say or how to react. I had too many questions. If he wasn't a caterer, that meant he had no clients, so where did the plant in Billy's hospital room come from? Why would he take the time to bring me to the market if he wasn't buying food? How did he come up with such elaborate descriptions of fake menu items for his fake catering jobs?

At the same time, other questions were answered. I finally understood why he drove rental cars and drove so slowly. He couldn't risk having his car spotted at the scene of a crime or being pulled over by the police for speeding. It had been important for Lori and I to keep our voices low because The Satchel Bandit had to wake up refreshed and ready to pull off his next heist. And I finally understood why he was so exhausted after his "church brunches." Instead of cooking all day, he drove five hours from Montreal to Toronto, robbed a bank, and drove right back. That's a long hike.

In retrospect, I should have been suspicious that a man who raved about his passion for cooking elaborate meals seldom made anything more complicated than nachos and guacamole when he was home with us. But he was an incredible storyteller. His catering tales were fascinating to me.

I heard my mother start to laugh.

"Are you okay?" I asked. I couldn't imagine what she found funny at that moment.

"His socks!" she said, giggling. "He didn't have his lucky socks this morning."

Lori and I started laughing, too.

I knew my mother felt embarrassed about being duped by Eddie, but it wasn't her fault. How could she have known the secrets he was hiding? He was a damn good liar, the best one yet. And for most of their relationship, she had focused her energy on trying to save Billy, making it easier for Eddie to slide by with his deceitful behaviour.

It was all so sickening to me. Doesn't anybody tell the truth, I wondered. It became clear to me that most men lied as easily as they breathed. Both my father and my stepfather had lived double lives. I was done trusting people. The only man I now felt I could trust had died before his twenty-second birthday. I immediately thought how horrible it would have been had Eddie been arrested while Billy was in the hospital. The news would have devastated him. My mother regretted putting Eddie's name on Billy's tombstone.

A few months later, Eddie was convicted on all forty-seven counts and given the maximum sentence of twenty-one years to be served at the Kingston penitentiary. My mother had their marriage annulled. I wrote him a letter. I wanted an explanation. He never responded.

Once the news came out, it was all everyone we knew could talk about. We were all shocked because Eddie did not seem like the bank-robbing type. Intelligent, charming men weren't supposed to rob banks. Embezzle from them, maybe, but not rob them at gunpoint.

Eventually, I learned the real reason Eddie had returned to Canada. He had done the same work in the U.S. and had spent time in prison. On release, he had no choice but to leave the country. One piece of information I found amusing was that he was in charge of cooking while he was in prison. I'm guessing there were no Cornish hens on that menu.

There was a newspaper article written about Eddie with the headline "Bored Businessman Robs 47 Banks for the Thrill." I suppose that was true. It certainly wasn't for the money. A police officer told my mom that Eddie would have made more money had he actually been a caterer. Bank robberies aren't huge scores unless you break into the vaults where the big money is kept. Equipped with only a toy gun and a pleasant demeanor, Eddie had to settle for whatever he could get from the teller. Even so, we couldn't help but wonder what he had been doing with the stolen money. My mom had her suspicions.

"Mexico," she told us, "I bet it's in Mexico."

A few months before his arrest, Eddie had suggested a family vacation. He let me, Lori and my mom offer suggestions, but ultimately the decision was his, and he chose Cancun. He told us it was because he loved the culture and the food. The reality was that in the 1980s, Canadians could fly to Mexico without needing a passport. Seeing as he was wanted by the police, Mexico was his safest option. While we were there, he would leave us at our hotel and go into town alone on mini-excursions. He explained that his fair skin was sensitive to the sun and prevented him from laying by the pool with the rest of us. He did this several times during that week.

After his arrest, my mother was convinced that the Satchel Bandit's loot was hidden somewhere in Cancun. We'll never know.

Although Eddie was out of our lives, he wasn't out of my mind. All of the lies and losses that I had experienced were weighing on me. I felt angry and vulnerable, and my self-esteem plummeted. It was hard for me to concentrate on school because that would mean believing in my future, something I found difficult to do.

Just one month after Eddie's arrest, I was dealt another blow when my mom was diagnosed with breast cancer. When she told us, I felt numbness flood my body. I wasn't emotionally capable of processing more bad news. Her voice sounded muffled, like she was speaking through a tunnel. Only a few words came through clearly: "It's early . . . simple procedure . . . I'll be okay."

This was not my mother's first breast cancer diagnosis; when this happened before, a lumpectomy and some radiation were enough to put her into remission for a few years. But even if she had gone through this before, she was in shock at its return. Billy hadn't been dead a year. She knew she needed to be healthy for Lori and me and was prepared to fight. Watching her go through her treatments drained me of whatever strength I had remaining.

I was expected to keep moving forward as if everything was fine, but it was just impossible. I was weak from my eating disorder. I was still grieving over Billy. I was hurt by Eddie and worried about my mom. If life wasn't going to give me a break, I decided, I had to take one for myself. The first step was dropping out of theatre school.

CHAPTER SIX

The Grip of a Disorder

I T WASN'T EASY TO GET ACCEPTED into the three-year program at The Dome theatre school in Montreal. I hadn't been sure that I had what it took, but I'd been desperate to get in. For my audition, I performed the Arthur Miller monologue Billy had suggested for me and I sang "Open Arms" by Journey. I am a terrible singer and I'm sure I destroyed the song, but they liked me enough to accept me into the program anyway.

The Dome offered a very different school environment than anything I had experienced before. In high school, everyone in my grade was the same age, and most of us shared similar backgrounds and upbringings. At the Dome, students in my class ranged from seventeen to twenty-five-years-old and came from everywhere, something I thoroughly enjoyed. Theatre school challenged me in ways that high school could not. I was constantly out of my comfort zone in classes on voice, makeup, and Shakespeare. In high school, we had been assigned to memorize a fourteen-line sonnet by Shakespeare. I got halfway through it before finding it too difficult and giving up. In theatre school, I learned the entire "To be or not to be" monologue from *Hamlet* with ease. It was exciting to discover new skills.

Initially, my grief over Billy and my eating disorder seemed to work to my advantage. It had only been a few months since Billy died, and my emotional numbness acted as a protective barrier between the pain of his loss and my responsibilities at school. Meanwhile, I had developed a co-dependent relationship with my eating disorder. It gave me a false sense of control, making me believe that I was strong and disciplined and that with its help I could survive anything. In the latter part of high school, like a lot of my friends, I smoked cigarettes and got drunk on weekends. In theatre school, I quit both, although doing so made me an anomaly among my friends for whom weed and drinking were popular habits. I wish I could say I was trying to be healthier but, in fact, I had quit drinking and smoking because I relished the feeling of self-control. Billy's death had taught me that my fate was out of my hands, but my body was mine to manipulate as I saw fit. The reality, however, was that the more restrictive I got with my diet and the more critical I became of my body, the more my life spun out of control.

My weight continued to drop at theatre school. My friend Lana found this disturbing.

"You look like a ten-year-old boy!" she yelled at me during a bus ride home. "Just eat a friggin' cookie, Marci!"

Lana never held back. She and I had become fast friends despite our differences. She was a six-foot tall brunette, a single child with an outrageous sense of humor and an inability to feel embarrassment. She always kept me laughing. We'd take our theatre games out of the classroom into the real world, playing catch on our bus rides with an invisible rubber ball. We would climb over people's laps and under their legs to catch it.

I managed to make it through the first year of school. Within a few months of the second year, however, I was finding it difficult to stay motivated. Once Eddie's conviction and my mom's cancer were added to the mix, I kept asking myself, "What's the point?" I didn't have a back-up plan. My high-school guidance counsellor had told me theatre is a tough business and I would need a Plan B, but I never wanted to consider any alternatives. I'd had faith in my destiny. Now, instead of wanting to stand up in front of the world, I wanted to hide from it.

My mother could see how withdrawn I was becoming and it worried her. The idea of me quitting the program saddened her, but she knew I was feeling crushed by the weight of events and wanted to support me. What she didn't know was that I was down on myself to the point where I was convinced that I wasn't talented enough or pretty enough to be successful and saw no point in forcing myself to keep trying. I quit school, thinking I would distance myself from the world for a while.

No longer having classes to occupy my mind, my focus shifted back to my weight. For the next few months, all I could think about was what I had eaten, what I was eating, and what I was going to eat. I rarely left my bedroom except to walk to the kitchen to pour myself cups of black coffee or to get the three apples I'd allow myself in a day. My body weakened but my eating disorder felt strong. I would stay up all night watching cooking shows and flipping through cookbooks. I obsessed over images of food but refused to eat. Staying up all night was my way of exhausting myself so I would sleep through most of the following day and avoid getting hungry. Watching me abuse my body was killing my mother and I was sure that it would eventually kill me too.

By this time, Lori was engaged and living with her fiancé. I lived with my mom in our apartment. One night, my heart suddenly felt like it was slowing down. I was positive it was finally giving out on me. "I'm going to die tonight," I thought, unsure of how I felt about it. Part of me found comfort in thinking I'd get to see Billy again, very soon. The other part of me was filled with guilt. The thought of my mother having to bury a second child was too much to bear. I kept thinking that I should get something to eat from the kitchen. I wanted so desperately to get my ass out of bed and eat something, anything! But as much as I feared hurting my mom, I feared gaining weight even more. I couldn't do it. I couldn't risk the extra calories without knowing for sure that they would save my life. I was willing to take my chances. I stayed up all night counting my heartbeats and monitoring their rhythm. Once the sun started to rise and I realized I had survived the night, I closed my eyes and drifted off to sleep.

"And sleep. That sometime shuts up sorrow's eye, steal me awhile from mine own company." I'd learned enough Shakespeare to know what to expect from sleep, but that wasn't what I got. My sleep was rarely ever peaceful. Oftentimes, I'd dream that I was eating something fattening and wake up

in a panic. Immediately, I'd reassure myself by running my hands along my hips to feel the bones protruding through my skin.

Despite all of the hours I'd spend in my bed, I was hardly relaxed. Many mornings, I'd wake up with my jaw locked shut from the tension that surged through my body. It was unpleasant but it gave me an excuse to avoid breakfast. My eating disorder could turn any kind of discomfort to its advantage. Stomach pains and lightheadedness were proof of my worthiness. On the rare days when I wouldn't feel physically ill, I'd assume I had overeaten and would cut more calories from my diet.

"It should have been me," the voice in my head still taunted me. How was I contributing to the world? What purpose was I serving by being alive? If Billy were here, he'd be doing great things. I was barely surviving and feeling miserable.

The weeks of sleepwalking through life turned into months. I thought it would go on forever but eventually I was ready to try to start living again. I knew that in order to do so, I'd have to leave Montreal. The reminders of everything I'd lost were too heavy for me to deal with. I needed to escape. Toronto was only five hours away by car, so it seemed the logical place to go. I decided to spend some time there to get a feel for the city. I called the only person I knew who lived there—my father—and made arrangements to spend the next few months with him.

My mother had concerns, naturally. My father had never been the most responsible parent. But she knew how miserable I was and wanted to be supportive, so she let me go.

My father lived in a rough area. The shopping center in his neighborhood was nicknamed 'Murder Mall' due to the amount of violence that happened there. When I got to his apartment, he told me to ignore the fire alarm that often went off in the night. "It's just the pimps roughing up their prostitutes in the stairway," he explained.

I slept on the couch and made sure I was awake and dressed before he woke up. I tried to make myself as little an inconvenience as possible. I had barely spent any time with him over the years, so our arrangement felt awkward. I didn't even know what to call him. I hadn't said the word 'dad' since he left us ten years earlier and was not about to start. Calling him by his first name felt a bit rude, so I did not call him anything at all. If we were watching TV and I had a question for him, I'd stare at him until he noticed. Once he looked in my direction, I'd ask.

My father was working as a stock boy for some packaging company. It was a far cry from owning a jewelry business, but he didn't seem to care. The first week I moved in with him, I got a job as a hostess at a restaurant. I needed a pair of pants and proper footwear so he took me to Murder Mall. As we were standing at the cash register, he realized he had forgotten his wallet at home and told me to cover the bill. I soon learned that forgetting his wallet was habitual for my father.

It took me three busses to get to work every day and two busses to get back—I walked the rest of the way to burn calories. I'd left a lot of things behind in Montreal, but not my eating disorder. Once back at the apartment building, I would skip the elevator and climb 121 stairs. On days when I was particularly anxious, I'd walk up and down the stairs three or four times in a row.

My father was a Type-1 Diabetic so he didn't keep sugar in the house, which was perfect for me. He did, however, stock up on a lot of alcohol. He was clearly still fond of it. It wasn't unusual for him to drink Scotch all night at his friend Jim's place across the hall.

It became clear after just a few weeks in Toronto that my experience was not going to be what I had hoped for. I wasn't learning much about the city, and I was learning more than I had bargained for about my father. My mother's concerns were justified. One night, he showed up at the restaurant where I worked, an hour before the end of my shift, and offered to drive me home. He was with his buddy, Jim. When I was finished and we were walking across the parking lot to his car, I heard a voice scream: "Marci! Do you know these guys?" It was the bartender. They had skipped out on their bill. I was mortified. My father apologized for the "oversight" and went back inside to pay. That night I imposed a new rule: never come to my workplace again.

The summer was supposed to be about me finding reasons to move forward with my life. Instead, I felt lonely and discouraged. I had done everything I could to make the situation work, from getting a job to landing a gig as an extra in a movie called *Where the Heart Is* starring Uma Thurman and Dabney Coleman. I'd thought the movie would be fun. It wasn't. We were dressed for summer and shooting in fall at a makeshift dump site. I was one of several extras protesting against the cold-hearted building developer played by Coleman. They brought out two industrial sized fans and threw garbage into them, which blew right at me and my fellow protesters.

After several hours of dodging garbage in the cold, I was exhausted, miserable, and ready to go home. My father was supposed to pick me up but he never showed. I called my mom the next morning. She wanted nothing more than to have me back home with her. Once again, my father and I were parting ways. This time, I was the one walking away.

As I grabbed my coat from the hallway closet, I noticed pictures of Lori, Billy, and me tucked away on the top shelf. I looked at my father as I walked out the door and said, "You lost your son, you'd think you'd want to hold onto your daughter." To which he replied, "You're not my responsibility."

Back with my mother, I felt a tidal wave of relief. No matter how scary life got, she was always my safe place to land. As disappointing as my experience with my father had been, it ended up fueling my desire to move forward and live a productive life.

I would move back and forth between Toronto and Montreal for the next couple of years, working as a waitress and a dance instructor. When I was in Toronto, my mom would regularly get on the train to visit me and we always had a great time together. My food and body image issues were still present, but when my mom was in town I relaxed and enjoy the meals we shared. With everything we had experienced to this point, we had become each other's safety nets and shoulders to lean on. She couldn't shield me from the challenges that life threw at me, but she did her best to make me feel loved and supported.

During one of my spells in Toronto, a friend of mine set me up on a date with someone whose name I recognized. The name was Nate.

Nate used to date a girl I knew. A few months before, my friend had shown him a dance workout video I had participated in, and I guess Nate liked what he saw. He told my friend that he was interested in meeting me. We chatted on the phone and agreed to go out on a date.

When I saw him, I recognized him instantly. He was still cute. He made a good first impression. We were only together a few minutes and I thought, "I could really like this guy."

CHAPTER SEVEN

Bring the Ring

"WE'RE EITHER GOING TO BE really good friends, or I'm going to marry you," Nate said confidently on our second date. We were eating pad thai and watching the seventies funk band Chunk o' Funk at The Bamboo Club.

"What did you say?" I mumbled back through a mouthful of noodles.

"I really like you," he said.

I really liked him, too, but it was only our second date and I was just getting to know him. Admittedly, it was nice to hear. At twenty-two, I hadn't had many boyfriends. I'd had my share of brief sexual encounters, but between my insecurities over my body and what I'd come to learn were my abandonment issues, I rarely let anyone get too close. I tried to convince myself that I didn't want a man in my life, when in reality I'd been starving for love since I'd lost my brother.

Nate already seemed different from other guys I had dated. He was goal-oriented and appeared to have his shit together. He seemed warm and sweet. He reminded me of Billy. There was also a familiarity between us, not only because we had met years earlier, but because we came from similar backgrounds. We were both children of divorced, liberal parents, and we shared the same relaxed views on religion. I liked to joke that I was more Jew-ish than Jewish, and he felt the same way. We'd also both had tragedy in our families. I'd lost my brother and he'd lost a close family member, although he was much younger and wasn't affected in the same way.

We continued to bond over our love of eighties music and action movies. There were a lot of differences between us, though. I was still following a strict vegetarian diet. He despised most vegetables and was allergic to fish. He loved beef. We presented to the world in opposite ways. He possessed a quiet cockiness and a conservative demeanour. I came across as a free-spirited, high-energy, wild child. In spite of these differences, or because of them, there was chemistry between us.

"Do I have to play it cool and wait a few days, or can I just ask you out again right now?" Nate asked when he dropped me off at the end of our second date. I admit I found his cockiness attractive. We set plans to meet a couple of days later. From there things moved quickly.

Three weeks into dating he invited me to his office Christmas party at the advertising agency where he had started a new job. I didn't own party clothes and wanted to buy something new to wear. I bought a killer catsuit, a slinky, body forming, one-piece jumpsuit with an embroidered V-neck neckline and a zipper going down the front with a big gold tassel at the end of it. I loved it.

We met at Nate's office. As soon as I removed my coat, his jaw dropped, but not in the way I was hoping for. He didn't say a word but the expression on his face asked, "What the hell are you wearing?" Clearly, he was expecting something business casual, classic pant suit or skirt and sweater combination. But I wasn't the business casual type. I could tell he was feeling anxious when we entered the party, worried what his colleagues would think. It turned out they loved me. The party was fun and his job was safe.

We continued to get closer. "Move in with me!" Nate said, before we'd even been dating three months.

"Okay!" I answered.

We were in our early twenties and naïve enough to think it was a good decision, and even a practical one. We moved into a tiny one-bedroom apartment in an old low-rise building. It was a tight squeeze for two people who were still getting to know each other but the transition went well. I started teaching fitness classes at a local gym and eventually became an assistant manager. I became an expert at promoting health and fitness to strangers while ignoring my own well-being.

Nate knew about my eating disorder but at the time we started dating, it had been laying low. Neither of us was overly concerned by it. That changed as soon as we moved in together. Our relationship was going well, but there was a part of me that felt unsettled and unsafe, making a perfect breeding ground for my disorder. It expressed itself differently now. My relationship with food became one of extremes. I would either eat way too much or not nearly enough. When I wasn't restricting, I was binging.

Not wanting Nate to find out, I tried to hide my struggle. On the days I wasn't working, I waited anxiously for him to leave for the office and then ran to the kitchen and grabbed the peanut butter and jam that had been occupying my thoughts since waking. Using a spoon, I ate from both jars and didn't stop until I felt ill. I put the spoon down to give my stomach a break. Once the pain and nausea subsided, I finished what was left in both jars.

The physical discomfort I felt was nothing compared to my shame and disgust. Terrified that Nate would learn what I had done, I walked to the grocery store and replaced the food I had eaten. I tried to remember how full the jars were when I had started eating, and scooped out enough to prevent him from noticing any difference.

The entire process was physically and emotionally exhausting, but my disorder had a hold on me that I couldn't break. I wasn't ready to fight it. I understood it well enough to know that as painful as it was, it was nowhere near as painful as what had created it. Instead of learning how to deal with the emptiness left by Billy's death and my other issues, I tried to fill it with food . . . or by avoiding food. I also hoped that being in a loving relationship could make me feel safe again.

"How do you feel about marriage?" Nate casually asked one night in bed.

"I dunno, how do *you* feel about marriage?"

"I'm not desperate to get married, but I'm not against it either," he said.

I felt the same way.

I've always been bothered by the stereotype of women as wedding-obsessed from the time they leave the womb until the moment they walk down the aisle wearing the gown they've always dreamed about. It's bullshit.

I wasn't sure I'd ever get married and, if I did, I didn't expect it to happen before I was thirty. But there I was discussing marriage at twenty-two with a man I'd known for ten months. I believed that neither of us, being the children of divorced parents, had unrealistic expectations when it came to love and relationships. We knew not to believe in fairy tales and happily ever after. But we were still hopeful that we would succeed. Our relationship was going well. We weren't madly in love with each other, but what does that mean anyway? We had fun together. I loved how we sang along to the car radio and laughed at the same jokes. We also shared open-minded views on social issues and our sex life was great. Was that love? It felt close. He was sweet and affectionate, and made me feel like he'd take care of me and protect my heart.

That night, we got engaged to be engaged. It was a secret we kept to ourselves until he could propose in a more traditional fashion with an actual engagement ring. That happened two months later during a vacation to the Dominican Republic, but I didn't make it easy for him.

Two weeks before our trip, knowing he was going to propose, I felt anxious. Were we too young? Was I ready for such a commitment? Billy's death had made it difficult for me to plan far in advance. Why bother making plans for a future so out of my control?

"Bring the ring," I said during moments of optimism, followed by "Don't bring the ring" when the worries flooded back. Ultimately, I told him to bring it.

A few days into our trip, as we were having drinks at the hotel bar, he dropped to one knee and asked me to marry him while a mariachi band played behind him. It was a fine proposal. I said yes. We called our families and celebrated with the new friends we had made on our trip.

Getting married was exciting, but the practical reality of it still scared me. It wasn't that I questioned my ability to commit to one person. It was that I was terrified of committing to the *wrong* one. The men I loved and trusted had a tendency to leave; it was either by choice or circumstance, but they always left. Deciding to give my heart to someone was daunting. While I knew it might be the answer I was looking for, I still had a nagging feeling that getting married meant setting myself up for more trauma. Staying single might protect me from more adversity. I knew I wasn't strong enough to handle more of that.

After hours of overthinking, I decided to push my fear aside and refocus my energy on all of the things that could go right instead of worrying about what could go wrong. All families went through challenges and obstacles. I assured myself that my future husband was a good man and we were going to make a great team and manage whatever came our way.

We set a date and planned our wedding, with our moms handling most of the wedding plans. We made it to the alter, but not without a glitch or two.

Six weeks before the big day, I took the train to Montreal for a girl's weekend with my best friend, Mickey. I stayed at her place. Our plan was to hit the old nightclubs we used to frequent, a last hoorah before I became a wife. Our plans got derailed, literally, when a truck driver got stuck on the tracks in front of my train. He abandoned the truck and jumped to safety. I was just standing up to go to the bathroom when the train hit the truck at full speed, thrusting me face first into the plastic food tray on the back of the seat in front of me. The lights on the train went black. I couldn't see anything but I could feel liquid rushing from my nose.

"Oh my God, oh my God, oh my God," I repeated to myself, trying to figure out what had happened.

"You're okay, dear, you're okay," said the elderly woman sitting next to me. But I knew I was not okay.

As one of the train crew members walked by, I called out, "I think my nose is broken!"

He handed me a few napkins for my bloody nose and told me to be patient. Fifteen minutes later, all of the passengers were instructed to get off the train, grab our bags from the luggage compartment and walk along the tracks to the closest station. It was a thirty-minute walk. I had no idea how I was going to make it with a bloody nose, carrying a heavy bag. That's when Canadian actor Saul Rubinek, came to my rescue, carrying my bag for me. I recognized him as soon as he tapped me on the shoulder to ask if I needed help. Once at the station, I was taken by ambulance to the hospital and treated. I got to Mickey's place at 2 a.m.

There were a lot of passengers on that train, but I was the only one injured. Instead of enjoying a weekend of girlfriend debauchery, I was stuck nursing a broken nose. Luckily, I was healed for my wedding day.

On June 5, 1994, I got married. The wedding was more formal than we would have liked, but it went well. From that day forward, it would be my husband and I against the world. We returned to Toronto to start our lives as husband and wife. We were optimistic, as young couples are. In our case, too much so.

PART TWO

TRAUMATISM

CHAPTER EIGHT

Newlywed Games

I SHOULD HAVE ENJOYED LIFE as a newlywed, but my eating disorder was raging. I was still cycling between binging and restricting and was desperate for help. My family doctor suggested a twelve-step program for food addicts. I was willing to try anything, and that program helped me get through the first big challenge of my new marriage.

"We're moving to the West Coast!" I announced to my mom. Nate had accepted a job at one of the larger marketing agencies in the country. She felt torn. She knew I didn't much like Toronto but was sad that I'd be living on the other side of the country. As always, she pushed her feelings aside to support me.

Moving far away from friends and family was both scary and exciting. I loved the idea of being able to start over in a new town. There, I wouldn't have to be Marci, the girl with the deal brother and criminal stepfather. I was just Marci. It felt liberating.

Life on the west coast turned out to be exactly what we needed, for a while. We were less than two years into our marriage and enjoying our new life together. My husband worked at the ad agency and I got a job at a café around the corner from where we lived. My job required me to show up at 5 a.m. to brew coffee and bake dozens of cinnamon buns before we opened an hour later. Waking up early was easy for me, so I'd make sure to get there half an hour earlier than I needed to; this gave me a chance to blast music through the café and take my time with my duties.

It was a small café, owned by a twenty-six-year-old entrepreneur who ran the shop during the day and fronted a punk band at night. He was a fabulous boss. Even though he created a relaxed working environment, my co-workers and I knew how seriously he took his business and we respected him for it. I was also lucky to work with amazing women who made me feel welcome from my very first day. We'd gotten into the habit of leaving each other funny notes and poems before shift changes, just to brighten each other's days.

My husband and I took advantage of the healthy, active lifestyle that west coast was known for. We hiked, biked, and rollerbladed regularly. We also discovered fairly quickly that we had very different ideas when it came to how we liked to spend our weekends. I wanted to get up early and start the day running; he preferred to sleep until noon, easing into the day. Our solution was for me to go to the gym or for a long walk as soon as I woke up, and then we'd meet for lunch a few hours later. It was perfect.

We were contestants on a game show, a modern version of *The Newlywed Game* called *Love Handles*, featuring radio personality Stu Jeffries as the host. We answered questions like, "Will your partner say you've ever forgotten his or her birthday?" And, "If you could make anything on your partner's body bigger, which part would you choose?" It was a cheap production but a fun experience, especially when we won! Our prize was a first-class train trip to Banff, Alberta. A few weeks later, through a fundraiser at his job, we also won a three-day trip to Las Vegas where we renewed our vows at the Elvis Chapel. He promised to "love me tender" and I promised to "never step on his blue suede shoes." Everything was fine until his next day back to work.

As soon as he came back home, he gave me the news: "They fired me." I was floored. I knew he wasn't getting along with his bosses, but I never thought they'd fire him so soon after moving us. We weren't sure what to do, but I knew I didn't want to move back to Toronto. Maybe it was being so close to the water and the mountains, or maybe it was just being in a new environment, but I felt good and my disorder was more or less under control. I was happy out west.

I got a second job as a night waitress at a bar. It wasn't easy. I wasn't used to working while he stayed home. He decided to use this time to write a novel. We weren't connecting as well as we had been. An attractive customer at my café asked me out for lunch and I was disturbingly tempted to accept, which is when my husband and I promised to make our relationship a priority again. After several months, he found another job. I left the cafe and started working at a women's only gym. Things felt a lot better in our marriage. We seemed settled.

Once my husband was back at work, I was ready for a new challenge. I wanted a baby. Up to that point, I had questioned whether or not I would ever be ready or selfless enough to be a mom. Then I woke up one morning desperate for the opportunity. I shared this revelation with my husband. He was all in. It was time to make a baby!

I was fortunate that my body let me know when I was ovulating, and I took full advantage of those days. One weekend, we invited some close friends over for dinner when my ovulation pains kicked in. Not wanting to miss the opportunity, I excused myself, went up to the bedroom, grabbed the biggest book on our shelf and dropped, creating a big boom.

"Hey, I need some help up here!" I yelled downstairs. My husband ran up to see what had fallen on the floor. Of course, the only thing on the floor was my underwear, which I had removed as I threw myself onto our bed, ready to be fertilized. After our quickie, we went downstairs and re-joined our friends.

A few weeks later, I was pregnant. The first thing I did was call my mom, who I spoke to several times a day. She was over the moon. Her baby was having a baby! Next, I surprised my husband by arranging M&M candies on the floor of our future nursery to spell 'Daddy.' He was thrilled.

I once read somewhere that a man becomes a father once the baby is born, but a woman becomes a mom the minute she decides to get pregnant. We have to prepare our bodies for the guest it will be hosting for nine months. I tried to eat well, exercise enough, and get the proper amount of rest. Despite my efforts, I suffered a miscarriage during my first trimester. I was devastated. The physical pain was nothing compared to the sadness I felt. Even though I wasn't very far along in my pregnancy, the emptiness was indescribable. My doctor assured me it wasn't my fault and that miscarriages are common, but I couldn't help but feel like my body had failed me. I was already falling madly in love with the little person I was creating and its loss took another piece of my heart.

The last thing I wanted to do that night was go to a concert, but we had tickets to see Prince, and I knew I needed to go, not for me, but for my brother. After he died, I promised myself that someday I would meet Prince and tell him about his biggest fan and how he was buried with *Sign o' the Times* in his casket. I had to keep my promise. Wearing something loose and comfortable, I dragged myself to the concert. I maneuvered my way through security and gave my letter to one of the roadies. I doubt if it made its way to Prince but I had to try. The concert was amazing and reminded me that Billy was always watching over me.

We got the green light from my doctor to try to again two months later. Once more, we conceived quickly. This time I simply called my husband at work to let him know that the four different pregnancy tests all confirmed that I was pregnant. I was happy, but also nervous. My mom was cautiously optimistic. We were both afraid of letting ourselves get too excited too soon.

Unfortunately, tempering our expectations didn't make things any easier when this pregnancy ended in a miscarriage, as well. The first miscarriage was horrible, but the second was worse. What if something was wrong with me? What if I'd never get pregnant?

It's amazing how aware you become of pregnant women around you when you're desperately trying to become one of them. It seemed like I was surrounded by pregnant bellies wherever I went. Feelings of grief draped me like a heavy blanket, draining my energy and my faith in becoming a mother. My doctor referred me to a fertility specialist named Dr. Wen, who told me he was fairly confident that I'd get pregnant again. I prayed that he was right.

CHAPTER NINE

Almost Unbeatable

A COUPLE OF MONTHS LATER, I was pregnant with baby number three. Dr. Wen put me on progesterone pills and told me not to over-exercise. I had fantasies of the perfect pregnancy experience where I would exercise right up until my first contraction and then jog to the hospital, hop on the delivery table, and pop out the baby. Instead, I was told to keep my workouts light, eat whatever I was craving, and allow myself to gain a few extra pounds. I wanted this baby very badly and was prepared to do whatever it took to bring the pregnancy to term.

"We're going to meet this one," my mom said when I told her I was pregnant again. "I can feel it. You're going to be holding this baby in your arms."

She couldn't explain why she was so optimistic, but something made her believe that everything was going to be okay. She became deeply invested in my pregnancy.

"Peanut butter and sardines!" she announced over the phone.

She was calling me at least twice a day to share with me *her* pregnancy cravings. According to mom, this was "our" pregnancy and she was making the most of it. My cravings were on the salty side; hers tended to be sweeter. I looked forward to her daily calls.

After my six-week ultrasound recorded a healthy heartbeat, we breathed easier and were able to relax. Even though my mom knew right away that I was pregnant, I waited until I had passed the three-month mark to tell the rest of our family and friends. I was still anxious but my mom reassured me and promised she would come out west and spend as much time with me as she could.

I was twenty-eight, the same age as my mom when she was pregnant with me. "Your father didn't want another baby but I was desperate for one more," she told me. "So, I seduced him on a camping trip and got my Marci!"

My pregnancy triggered for mom memories of my early childhood and I enjoyed listening to her stories. Lori and Billy had been born two years apart. I had come along five years later. My mom adored all of us equally but with my older siblings at school all day, she said that she especially enjoyed her time alone with me. She relished being a mom and was damn good at it, surprisingly so considering the parents who raised her. My mother was the youngest of three girls. When she was born, her father, who had wanted a son, waited four days before going to the hospital. If my mom or her sisters raised their voices, my grandmother would yell, "I hope you get throat cancer!" My mother decided at a young age that when she had children, she would be the mother that she wished she'd had.

We didn't only have those early years together; after Billy died and Lori moved out, it was just the two of us again, me and my mom against the world. She was my "Mamacita" and I was her "Sunshine". We considered ourselves an unbeatable team. At random times of the day, she'd turn to me and say, "Un", I'd answer, "Beat", and together we'd say, "Able!" Unbeatable!

Four and a half months into my pregnancy, I arrived home after a positive ultrasound of my baby boy and heard the phone ringing. It was my sister. I was excited to hear her voice. I was heading to Montreal at the end of the week and looked forward to sharing the ultrasound pictures with her and everyone else.

"You need to come home now. Mommy's dying," she said.

My mind went blank for a moment and then flooded with questions but, as usual, all I could say was "What?"

I was aware that her breast cancer had come back two years earlier but she had led me to believe that her treatment was going well. It turned out she had lied, and I understood why. After watching me suffer two miscarriages, she didn't want me worrying about her health. But shielding me in this way hadn't helped when Billy was dying, and it didn't help now. I felt completely blindsided.

"When?" I asked.

"She won't make it to Friday. Get here as soon as you can," Lori said matter-of-factly.

I booked the next available flight home. Nate arranged to meet me in Montreal the following day. My mother was on a palliative care unit which was very different from the other floors. There was wine available in the guest area and smoking was permitted in the rooms. Since nobody admitted to this floor would leave, the patients were free to spend their last days doing what they wanted. Most of the patients understood their fate and had accepted it. My mother was not one of them. She was not ready to die.

When I walked into her room, I was overcome. The woman I had known with big auburn curls, chiseled cheekbones, and perfect skin . . . looked frail. The cancer had spread to most of her bones and organs. Her face was swollen and her skin was jaundiced. The cherry popsicle she nibbled on explained the deep pink color of her lips, but I recognized the red that covered her gums and teeth as blood from the breakdown of her liver. I had seen the same thing with Billy. I wanted to jump into bed with her and have her wrap her arms around me the way she did after my father abandoned us, when I slept in her bed for a full year. I wanted her to tell me everything was going to be okay. It was my mother who had helped me through all of my losses. Who was going to help me with losing her?

I sat by her bed and held her hand for hours. We looked at the ultrasound pictures together and I listened to her talk about her plans to travel to the west coast to spend time with her grandson. I was swept up in her fantasy until the beep of a monitor or interruption from a nurse snapped me back to reality. Later that night she slipped into a coma.

When we got to the hospital the next day, the doctor told us that although she was could not speak, she was able to hear us. We were encouraged to talk to her as much as possible. Finding the right words to say was incredibly challenging. I was not ready to say goodbye. As selfish as it was, I needed her to stay alive for me. I was not prepared to live the rest of my life without her.

I knew she would worry about me feeling lost without her, so I assured her that I'd be okay. I was lying. The truth was that I felt like a toddler who had lost her mom in a crowd. I would spend the rest of my life feeling scared and alone. But I lied to protect her, the same way that she had lied to protect me.

There had always been music playing in our house, and my mom had been a huge Frank Sinatra fan. When I spotted a CD player in the corner of the room and a Sinatra CD on the shelf next to it, I put it on. I pressed play and started to walk back across the room only to hear Frank's voice singing "And now, the end is near, and so I face, the final . . ."

Mortified, I flew across the room like Tom Cruise and silenced the machine. I switched the CD to Aretha Franklin and prayed she hadn't noticed my fuck-up. Lori and I stayed late into the night before going back to her house to get some rest. We waited until my mom's boyfriend got there before we left. She had been with him for the past nine years. He was the warm and loving man she had always wanted and deserved. It was comforting to know that she had finally experienced a healthy, loving relationship.

Back at my sister's place, I climbed into bed and read Dr. Seuss' *Oh, Baby, The Places You'll Go* to my pregnant belly, the way I did every night. I spoke to the baby in my belly and told him how much his bubby loved him, even though she wouldn't be there to meet him in November. I was still awake when I heard the phone ring. It was my mom's boyfriend telling us to rush back to the hospital. We got there as fast as we could but not soon enough to see her take her last breath.

That was it. My mom was gone. What do you do with all of the love you have for someone once they're gone? Where does it go? My hands went to my belly as I tried to focus my love on my son. I looked up and saw Nate walking towards me. He had taken a cab straight from the airport when his flight landed. It was good to see him. We left the hospital and drove out of the city to stay at my sister's place. Sitting in her living room at 2 a.m. writing our mother's obituary felt surreal. Reminiscing about our mom was both heartbreaking and soothing. Her loss was devastating, but her impact on my life had been pure joy.

At the time of her death, she had $1,000 to her name, which we put towards her modest funeral. After her second-to-last bout with breast cancer, she had used her money to open a lingerie store that catered to women with a history of breast cancer. Boutique Image Feminine specialized in bra fittings for women who had undergone mastectomies. It was also a place where women came to buy a pretty nightgown and ended up staying for hours to talk with my mom. She had a gift for making people feel safe and loved. It wasn't until after she died that I found out she had given a portion of everything she sold to the Canadian Breast Cancer Foundation, where she also worked as a volunteer. She was dead at fifty-six years of age with so much more to give, and so many more lessons to teach me.

I was, however, grateful for some of the wisdom passed on to me:

1. Nobody is inferior or superior to anyone else.
2. It doesn't matter what religion you practice, as long as it helps you be a kinder person.
3. It's important to let yourself have mini-breakdowns once in a while, because the little ones keep you from the big, destructive ones.
4. When it comes to relationships, if there's a problem in the bedroom, there's probably a problem outside of the bedroom. Figure out what the real issue is and fix it.
5. Dance and sing, even if you're horrible at both.
6. When it comes to your health, do not let yourself be dismissed or ignored by doctors. If you believe there is something wrong, fight to be heard. Be your own advocate.

The last one would prove to be life-saving. I don't remember much leading up to her funeral or from the days that followed it. I remember Lori planning everything. She was tougher than I was and, as the older sibling, she was comfortable taking charge. My mom had said that she wanted a small, private funeral, and that's what she got.

Nate flew back home after the funeral and I stayed on a few more days. On the flight back, I wore a new maternity dress I had gotten as a gift from my mother-in-law.

I sat in an aisle seat, trying to keep my emotions in check, wondering how I could ever be a mother without my mother, when a flight attendant leaned over to pick up the coffee cup of the passenger next to me. She accidently spilled its contents all over my brand new, powder blue cotton dress. I immediately started to cry. The flight attendant was neither impressed with my reaction nor apologetic for her mistake. She looked at me snidely and said, "It's just coffee, it's not a big deal."

I stopped crying long enough to look her in the eyes and say, "My mother just died. My father abandoned me, my brother's dead, my stepfather is in jail, I've had two miscarriages and my sister and I barely speak. I'm also pregnant with my first child. That's why I'm crying."

I realized afterwards that what I blurted was lot for anybody to digest, even a snotty flight attendant. She mumbled, "Oh, sorry," and walked away.

I spent the rest of the flight wondering how I was going to cope. My usual strategy would have been to starve myself so I could have a sense of control over the situation, or binge eat to offset my feelings of abandonment. Being pregnant, I couldn't do either. I would have to suppress my grief until my baby was born and then let myself feel it.

I promised my baby that I would do everything I could to make sure he always felt loved and protected. As always, life had a way of making me prove it.

CHAPTER TEN

Trauma Upon Trauma

"TWINS?" THE ELDERLY WOMAN ASKED, pointing to my belly.

"Um, nope. Just one," I said.

"I think there are two in there," she continued. "You're so big!"

While I was surprised by her brazen remarks, I didn't disagree. Dr. Wen had already told me that I was going to have a big baby.

Normally, being told I looked huge would have been upsetting, but as I waited for a taxi to bring me to the hospital, I had more serious things on my mind. After losing my mom three months earlier, I had become overly anxious about my pregnancy. Every week I went into different health clinics to check my baby's heart rate and make sure he was okay. At one clinic, a nurse left my chart open when she left the room, allowing me to read the words "neurotic mother" under my name.

I thought that was a bit harsh. Yes, I was anxious about my pregnancy, but my concerns didn't keep me from enjoying it. Luckily, my eating disorder had given me a reprieve during those eight months so I could take full advantage of the weird food cravings I was having. My husband was surprised yet supportive when I called him at work one day and told him I wanted chicken soup with matzo balls for dinner. His vegetarian wife was asking for chicken soup. He came home with a boatload of it. I also drank can after can of clamato juice and ate jars of olives every single day. This baby loved salt.

Everything was smooth until I was thirty-four weeks into my pregnancy and stopped feeling the baby move. He wasn't a big kicker, but he liked to swim. Nate and I laughed hysterically as my belly rolled side to side whenever the baby changed positions. I was so used to his activity that I knew something was wrong when it stopped. I researched baby books that suggested drinking orange juice and listening to music to wake him. I still felt nothing. I waited a few hours before giving in to panic and headed to the hospital.

As soon as I got to emergency, I asked for a Nonstress test to check my baby's heart rate. They denied my request. I was floored. It was a teaching hospital and, apparently, at the very beginning of my pregnancy, I had agreed to be part of a study that made me ineligible for that particular test. Were they kidding me? I didn't remember agreeing to anything, and I was furious. The nurse explained that the test she'd be administering instead was actually better at detecting any possible problems. I wasn't happy but felt I had no choice.

The test I was given showed no reason for concern, and I was told to go home and rest. I wasn't comforted by these words and still felt in my heart that something was wrong. I didn't want to leave and all of my worry and panic turned into uncontrollable sobbing. Unsure of how to handle me, the nurse left my side and returned with a doctor. I disliked him immediately. His skin was too tanned, his hair too coiffed, his teeth too white. He looked like an actor playing a doctor on a soap opera. Through a huge, insincere smile, Dr. Smarmy took my hand, looked into my eyes and said, "You're fine."

That was it? That was supposed to make me feel better? I was still a crying mess. I told him I needed more tests. Once again, he looked into my eyes and said, "If, in a week from now, you're still concerned, come back. But I can promise you, your baby is fine."

I cried all the way home. I kept talking to my belly and praying I'd feel some movement, but I felt nothing. I was awake most of the night. As soon as the sun came up, my mother's words came rushing back to me: "When it comes to your health, fight to be heard. Be your own advocate."

"I'm going back to the hospital!" I told my husband as he got ready for work, "I'll call you from there."

When I walked into the emergency room, I was greeted by an intern who looked like Doogie Howser M.D. This time I didn't ask for the test I wanted, I demanded it. He knew better than to argue with a pissed-off pregnant woman and found a more experienced doctor to deal with me, a perinatologist visiting from the east coast. He listened to my concerns and took them seriously. An ultrasound followed by the Nonstress test validated my concerns. My baby wasn't moving. Something was wrong.

The specialist said that he didn't know what the problem was, but believed the safest course of action would be an emergency C-section. He was less concerned with the baby being six-weeks premature than he was with whatever was causing the lack of movement. I called my husband as they prepared me for surgery and told him that his son was on the way.

They waited for the epidural to kick in before performing the surgery. I found it agonizing to watch the monitor and see his heart rate drop. I wanted them to rip me open and get him out before it was too late. My husband arrived, calm and focused, just as things were getting started. I could feel them pulling and tugging and I prayed that we weren't too late.

"He's out!" the doctor said, lifting him up to give me a quick look. "He's alive but he's in trouble."

He squeezed my hand, smiled kindly, and then gave his attention to the baby, who looked small and pale.

They explained that my placenta had separated, causing my baby to leak out seventy-five percent of his blood. Without blood, there's no oxygen. At that point, they couldn't tell if it had been a slow leak or a fast one. His chances of survival were better with a slow leak, making the loss of oxygen less dramatic. The doctor told us that while the paleness of his skin was concerning, white skin was better than blue and he promised to do everything he could to keep him alive.

As I lay in the recovery room, a nurse told me how lucky I was to have arrived when I did. "If you had waited another hour, you would have lost him for sure," she said.

Immediately, I thought of how Dr. Smarmy had told me not to come back for a week. I had never wanted so badly to punch someone. Then I thought of my mom. She was the reason I came back. She had saved my baby's life.

My mom had learned to stand up for herself a few years earlier after a routine mammogram. She had called her doctor for the results and was told by the receptionist that everything was fine, that the shadow on her breast was nothing to be concerned about. "Shadow? What shadow?" my mother asked, before requesting to speak with the doctor directly. He was the same doctor who had treated her since her first diagnosis at age thirty. He had performed her mastectomy. She realized that he had kept this information from her.

"You've had it for years, it's nothing" he told her flippantly. "I've seen this type of thing a million times." But my mother disagreed. She was furious that he had withheld information from her. She made an appointment to meet him in person. During the appointment, she requested a biopsy that he refused to perform. Once again, he told her that he'd seen it before and was positive that it was nothing to be concerned about. When she persisted, he accused her of wasting his time and overreacting.

She asked him, firmly, to write on a piece of paper "This is not cancer" and sign his name. When he refused, she requested a biopsy again. This time, he grudgingly agreed.

The results of the biopsy were positive for a malignancy. She had cancer again and it had spread to her bones. She died two years later. The cancer killed her, but I consider her doctor's arrogance its accomplice. It was after this final diagnosis that she made it her mission to ensure that Lori and I understood the importance of fighting for our health and standing up to doctors. She had been gone for three months and was still empowering and protecting me.

My son was treated in the neonatal intensive care unit while I recovered on the maternity ward. A nurse walked in and noticed my mom's picture on my bedside table.

"Is that your mom? Is she on her way over?" she asked.

"I wish, but she died three months ago," I answered honestly.

The nurse froze before bolting out of the room. She came back twenty minutes later and apologized for her reaction, explaining that she hadn't been prepared for it. I understood. I wasn't prepared for any of this either. Being in the maternity ward without a baby is tough. I heard all the mothers talking and singing to their crying and cooing babies, while I sat by myself, waiting for updates about my son. My husband called our friends and family to let them know what was going on.

I sat wondering, "What the fuck did I do?" I must have done something terribly wrong in a past life to warrant the shit I was catching in this one. I honestly believed that I wouldn't survive another blow. If I lost this baby, I was done. There would be more people loving me from heaven than there would be on earth. The thought of being with them was more comforting than being here without them. But right now, the baby was alive and fighting, so I had to be strong and fight in just the same way.

Nate and I spent as much time in the neonatal intensive care unit as we were allowed. Our baby was given two blood transfusions. We couldn't see him while he was recovering. When he was finally strong enough to be held, I was introduced to "kangaroo care," and it was glorious. Studies had proven incredible health benefits from skin to skin contact between sick babies and their parents. I sat topless behind a curtain, with my naked preemie pressed up against my chest so our hearts beat together. It was an incredible feeling, as healing for me as it was for him. Our son amazed his doctors with how quickly his health turned around. He was out of the hospital in two weeks.

We were excited when we brought him home but had no clue how to care for him. We placed him on the floor in front of us and looked at each other and said, "What now?"

I held my baby as much as I could. Even though he was doing well, he was still too weak to breastfeed, so I pumped my milk and bottle-fed him. I had enough milk to feed triplets, a tough situation when your baby isn't eating much. Another aspect of being premature was that my son wouldn't wake himself up to eat the way full-term that babies do. We had to wake him every four hours to feed him. We took turns. It was a long process. We would wake him, turn on the light, switch on the radio, and feed. The lights and music kept him from falling asleep before he was done. By the time he was finished, it would almost be time to feed again. I was exhausted. My husband was too. We were parenting zombies. I was so tired that I forgot to attach the bottle to the breast pump machine, and pumped my milk all over myself and my sheets.

Nate's parents and my sister tried to help and they meant well, but we had very different ideas about what I needed. They wanted to keep their days free and help me at night. But I had my husband home with me at night and needed company while I was alone during the day. Fortunately, I found a mom-and-baby group which I attended on Thursdays. I hung out with other new moms and got some support. I invited my mother-in-law to accompany me. She said yes but wound up changing her mind. I missed my mom terribly.

What should have been a bonding experience between my in-laws and me instead drove a wedge between us. They adored their new grandson and wanted the best for their son, but my well-being wasn't as important to them. They told me I was unfair when I wanted to order some take-out for dinner instead of going out. Their son had been at work all day and deserved a good meal. I still hadn't mastered breastfeeding and was more comfortable doing it at home. I was also tired.

Once his parents and my sister had left and it was just the three of us again, we found our groove. Our baby was doing great and hitting all of his milestones. I still struggled with not having my mother with me to experience all of this, but I was determined to apply everything I had learned from her to be the best mother I could.

* * *

Between our child's traumatic entrance and the stressful relationship with my in-laws, my eating disorder was slowly and subtlety finding its way back. Having a baby can be challenging on any women's self-esteem, but when you've been battling an eating disorder for ten years, it's inevitable. I started exercising as soon as my stitches had healed and followed a diet consisting of yogurt for breakfast, two rice cakes with fat free cream cheese for lunch, and salad with tuna for dinner. The weight started to come off. Having control over my diet gave me the usual false sense of control over my life, which I needed to help me get through what happened next.

It had been almost a year since my mother's death and it was time for her unveiling. I expected this would be difficult for me. I had been in shock during her funeral so I didn't feel the full impact of her death. Now, a year later, I would be standing at her gravesite, looking at her tombstone after having spent the last 365 days missing her terribly.

"I'm making your mom a surprise party" my father-in-law told my husband few weeks before the unveiling.

"What the fuck is he talking about?" I asked.

Since the unveiling was the same month as my mother-in-law's birthday, my father-in-law thought it made perfect sense to have both events the same week. I did not share his feelings. The worst part was that we would be staying at my in-law's house, where the party was taking place. When we flew into town two weeks later, I had no idea what to expect, but my gut told me it was going to be a shit show.

My gut was right. The night we got there, my husband went out with his brothers and his best friend while I stayed in with the baby and spent most of the night in our bedroom trying to avoid my in-laws. I'd encouraged the boys to go out because I wanted Nate to spend time with his younger brother, who he didn't get to see much. I didn't expect him to crawl into bed drunk at 3 a.m. after spending hours at a strip club. I wasn't impressed.

The baby woke me up a few hours later while Nate slept in. The house was filled with excitement over the upcoming party. My older brother-in-law and his family had just arrived in town and were also staying at the house with us. Nobody understood why I wasn't in a party mood. I recognized that they were there to celebrate their mom. Why couldn't they respect that I was there to mourn mine?

"It's been almost a year. Why isn't she over it yet?" my brother-in-law asked Nate over dinner one night.

"Why are you in such a bad mood?" my sister-in-law wondered. "You're acting like such a bitch!"

I was in a house full of people and I couldn't have felt more alone.

The unveiling, much like the funeral, was private and quiet. I don't care what the cliché says, time does not heal all wounds. My wounds were deep, and healing hadn't even started.

Soon after came the birthday party. Despite the pressure I was under to put on a happy face and join the festivities, I couldn't do it. I stayed in my bedroom with my baby for most of the night, reading books and singing songs. He was my family. I brought him downstairs briefly to introduce him to some of the relatives. Nate, who liked to avoid conflict with his mom, spent most of the night celebrating with his family. We were two days away from heading back home and I was counting the hours.

The following night, while we were getting ready to go to sleep, Nate brought up the idea of opening our marriage to having sex with other people.

"Excuse me?" I asked him.

"I think it could be cool to mix up our sex life by bringing in other people" he continued. "What about you? What are your fantasies?"

I love sex and we enjoyed a healthy sex life. But . . . holy shit. He wanted me to choose a friend of his that I would sleep with. I wasn't having it. I'm not sure which part of what I was going through made his suggestion feel the most insensitive to me. Was it the fact that we'd just been to my mom's unweiling or the fact that I had just recently given birth to his first child after two miscarriages and maybe didn't have any desire to share my body with anybody else? In any case, my answer was no.

It was finally time to go home. I had traveled with a dream baby on the flight in, but the poor kid started teething on the flight back. He screamed the entire length of the flight. By the time we walked through our front door, I was exhausted but relieved to be back.

For the next four months, we continued with our regular routine. During the day, my husband went to work and I took care of the baby. At night, we'd hang out together watching TV and listening to music. Things were still uncomfortable with me and his family and I felt a little betrayed by his choice to stay neutral. We had promised each other we'd be a team, but I guess some boys just don't want upset their moms.

One beautiful August weekend, we took our son for a weekend getaway to the islands. While we were at the hotel, my husband and I got caught up in a moment of friskiness and had a quickie while the baby napped. A month later, on his first birthday, I found out I was pregnant again. Who knew it would be that easy this time? It was pregnancy number four for me. We decided that having two babies so close in age would be a bit challenging without support. We also didn't like the idea of our kids growing up away from their cousins and grandparents. Despite my relationship with my in-laws, I wanted our kids to be close to them. We made the difficult decision to move back east.

Our plan was to move back and get settled before the baby was born. But when had anything in my life gone as planned?

CHAPTER ELEVEN

And Then Worse

"LET ME GO! PLEASE LET ME GO!" I begged my nurses while pulling at the intravenous lines in my arms. "My baby needs me! Please let me go home!"

I felt hands grab my wrists and tie them to the bed. The restraints were pulled tight to make sure they were secure.

"Calm down, Marci" one of my nurses said softly but firmly. "You need to calm down."

This was the first of many times I would try to extubate myself in an effort to escape from the hospital.

I found it hard to believe that just two weeks earlier, I was at home with a sixteen-month-old child, listening to music and talking to him about my pregnant belly and his sibling who was growing in it. We were progressing on the move back east. My husband had quit his job and been rehired at his old firm in Toronto. I was anxious because we hadn't found a place to live yet. He told me to stop worrying so much. We had enlisted the help of a few friends to help us find a place to live and he said we'd find something quickly.

I was five months into this pregnancy and things were going well. We hadn't been told the gender of the baby yet, but I *knew* I was having another son. My husband's genes made boys. At that point, there hadn't been a girl born into his family in over sixty years. That was fine with me. I loved the idea of raising brothers and couldn't wait for my son to meet his new friend.

The baby was due on our six-year wedding anniversary. It was the best gift either of us could imagine.

I had just spent ten days on antibiotics for a sinus infection and was finally feeling well again. I had been hesitant about taking medication while I was pregnant, but my doctor assured me that erythromycin was safe. My husband and I were lying in bed when my stomach started rumbling and grumbling loudly. The noises were hilarious and we joked about how annoying it must be for the baby.

The circus in my tummy kept me up most of the night. Then the pain started. As soon as I started getting out of bed, I was hit with horrible belly cramps. I set myself back down and waited for it to pass. My immediate concern was for the baby. I called Dr. Wen's office and arranged to see him later that morning. The pain came in waves and I tried to stay optimistic every time it subsided. Dr. Wen checked the baby's heart rate as well as my vital signs and told me that everything looked fine. He suggested I ease up a bit with my activity and get more rest.

I remembered that the day before, after grocery shopping, I had carried heavy grocery bags into the house. I carried all five bags at the same time instead of making two trips and was worried that I caused the pain I was experiencing. Dr. Wen assured me that the baby was fine and told me to go home and relax.

That night, things got worse.

The pain became excruciating. I made it to morning and my husband took me to the hospital. The doctors could not figure out what was causing my pain. They decided to keep me overnight for observation. During an ultrasound, I asked the technician if she could tell me my baby's gender. They had very strict rules about not revealing the gender of the fetus before the third trimester, so she apologized and said no. I looked at her pleadingly and said, "I lost two babies. I really want to connect to this one. I believe I am having another boy. Can you just confirm if I'm right?"

The technician gave me a sly smile and said, "I'm sorry, I can't give you that information," while nodding her head up and down . . . clearly symbolizing that I was having a baby boy. I was excited to know that I'd be meeting him in a few months.

I was relieved to hear that everything appeared to be normal despite the pains I was experiencing. I got back to my room and tried to relax when a nurse walked in. She had just finished her shift and popped in to ask me if I needed anything. She could tell that I was worried about the pregnancy and chatted with me for several hours. Her demeanour was calming and comforting. Before she left, she suggested that I write my unborn son a letter. She explained that it would help me feel more connected to him. I took her suggestion.

In my letter, I told him how much I was looking forward to meeting him. I also talked about the love that was waiting for him from his dad and big brother. I promised to keep him safe.

"I'll always do everything in my power to protect you," I wrote.

Writing the letter was helpful. It reminded me of the strength I had inherited from my mom and how I needed to tap into it to get through this challenge. The next day I was sent home with strict orders to cut my daily activity in half. It was considered "partial bed rest," and Nate and I hoped it would solve the problem.

I was home for less than twenty-four hours before he had to rush me back to hospital. The pain was worse. Something was very wrong. Being a teaching hospital, it wasn't properly equipped to deal with my situation, so I was taken by ambulance to a different hospital. They conducted test after test to determine what was happening, all to no avail. My blood pressure was shockingly low and my white blood cell count was terrifyingly high. My body was battling an infection but the doctors had no idea what kind. They needed to perform exploratory surgery in hopes of getting a diagnosis before the infection became fatal. I underwent a laparoscopy, which was considered a minimally invasive procedure to look at my organs. The doctors were still stumped and I continued to get sicker. I was constantly asking about the condition of my baby and was relieved to hear that he was still doing well. The pain was intense as I lay in bed with bags of fluid draining from the incision sites on my stomach. I spoke to the baby as much as I could, promising him that I'd fight to keep us both alive.

Still without a diagnosis and my condition plummeting, the next step was a laparotomy. This time they cut my pregnant belly completely open so they could see exactly what was going on inside. In the recovery room after the surgery, I asked a nurse, "Do they know what it is?"

She said that they did.

Then she said, "How are you smiling? You must be in tremendous pain!"

I explained that if the doctors had figured what was wrong, they could start treating me and save my baby. That made me happy.

What was wrong with me was called Clostridium Difficile (C-Diff), a bacterial infection that attacks the bowels. It was a gift from the antibiotic that I had taken for my sinus infection. The antibiotic had killed the bad bacteria from my sinuses, but allowed the C-Diff to grow. This isn't an uncommon reaction to wide spectrum antibiotics like erythromycin, but being pregnant threw my doctors off the trail.

In that moment, I thought I was safe. I thought my baby was safe. What I didn't realize was how far the bacteria had progressed and how much of my body it had destroyed. The surgeon told me that my insides resembled a tiger: they were black and orange with bacteria. Knowing what was killing me was helpful, but stopping it from killing me was going to be harder than they had hoped.

I was given heavy doses of strong antibiotics to battle the C-Diff as well as copious amounts of pain medication. I kept asking about my baby, who was still doing well despite the madness in my body. He was a strong little boy, just like his big brother. I thought I was strong, too, but I was getting weaker. The bacteria caused my organs to shut down, resulting in renal failure. At that point, I was transferred to the Step-down Unit of the hospital where the nurse to patient ratio was 1:3.

Between the illness and the medications, I was losing the ability to communicate with the people around me. My sister flew in from Montreal despite having just given birth to her third child. I couldn't speak so she was given a piece of paper with the alphabet written on it. When I wanted to speak, she would hold the paper in front of me so I could spell out the words by pointing to each letter one at a time. It didn't work. Despite my best efforts, I pointed to the spaces between the letters and we both ended up frustrated.

The renal failure caused swelling in my feet that soon made its way up the rest of my body. This made it impossible for me to close my legs or sit in a chair. I couldn't find a position that was comfortable, and the pain in my stomach was still intense.

Nate was by my side from the beginning. He would sit at my bedside all day and leave when they kicked him out at night. We were lucky to have made a few close friends in town who took care of our child while we were both at the hospital. I missed my little boy tremendously. Before I had gotten sick, I hadn't spent a single day away from him, and now it had been a couple of weeks since I'd seen his face or heard his voice. It was agonizing.

My mind was becoming cloudy from the strong mix of medications. My thoughts were muddled and I started to experience hospital-induced psychosis. One minute I was completely aware of where I was, but the next I was living in an alternate universe that was violent and threatening.

The delusions came out of nowhere and the scenarios constantly changed. At one point, I believed that I was lying in the infirmary at a national park. I was there because I had been viciously raped and the police were having a hard time reaching me. In the bed next to me was my rapist, who had gotten injured during the attack. I tried desperately to tell the nurses in charge that he was going to attack me again, but when I tried to speak, no sound come out. I lay there terrified and in pain.

My husband watched helplessly as I yelled and cried for help. He tried to reassure me that I was safe but couldn't get through to me. I baffled him by trying to climb out of my hospital bed, because I was convinced that I had killed a group of teenagers by drinking and driving. He kept reminding me that I didn't drive a car or drink alcohol. Guilt ridden, I was determined to turn myself in to the authorities and accept my punishment. I have no idea how long these delusions lasted. It could have been minutes, hours, or even days. I was losing control of my body and my mind.

One day, a nurse ran into the hallway to get my husband because I had called out a name she didn't recognize. It was Billy. I was calling out for my big brother. Did I see him? Was I yelling for him to protect me? I'd love to know what was going through my head. I'd like to think that he was watching over me the way he always had.

The swelling from my renal failure got to the point where nurses were having difficulty finding veins to use for my IVs. The ones in my arms were blown and unusable. They tried to go through my foot but weren't successful and ended up using a vein in my neck. On the afternoon of February 1, one of the doctors gave me a diuretic to try and release some of the fluid that was filling my organs. That proved to be a very bad decision. It sent me into shock. Seconds before they lost my pulse, I turned to Nate and asked him to kiss our baby goodbye for me.

I don't know how long it took to revive me, but in that short period of time, my baby, my strong little fighter, couldn't hang on any longer. He lost his fight. I lost my son. But I didn't yet know it. I spent the next two days heavily sedated and barely coherent. He was dead, but he was still in my womb. It was a dangerous situation because my body was still working hard to carry him and that was draining me. A C-section wasn't a safe option because of my fluid imbalance. The longer he stayed inside me, the weaker I became. My husband was told that if I didn't go into labour in the next day or two, a hysterectomy could be required. I'm glad I was oblivious to that conversation.

Two days later, I started having contractions, but I was still too out of it to know I was in labour. It was 2 a.m. on February 3 when the baby was delivered. I never got to hold him or even see him. One of the nurses called my husband to let him know what happened but suggested he get more sleep before coming back in the morning. The nurse told him that the baby was beautiful and looked just like his brother.

* * *

It was several days before I fully comprehended that I wasn't pregnant any longer. When I woke up, I asked about my baby and passed out again. I did this repeatedly for days. Once I understood that he was gone, I was not ready to accept the loss and completely avoided talking about it. I couldn't handle it so I temporarily put the reality of the situation on hold. Not only was I not emotionally stable enough to deal with losing my baby, but my physical condition was deteriorating. The swelling had reached my throat and made it impossible for me to breathe on my own. I woke up one morning and discovered I had been transferred to the Intensive Care Unit and put on a ventilator.

"You're weird," was the first thing I heard when I opened my eyes and saw Dr. Wen. "People your age don't die from C-Diff!" I loved Dr. Wen. I'd always found his straightforward yet kind demeanor comforting. I didn't blame him at all for not catching the C-Diff. It was an easy thing to miss in my case.

My case was rare and the whole hospital talked about the unfortunate, twenty-nine-year-old pregnant mother who was dying from having taken an antibiotic for a sinus infection.

Being in the ICU was traumatizing. I was terrified every minute of the seventeen days I spent there. I had never felt so vulnerable and unsafe in my life, despite the fact that the nurse to patient ratio was now 1:1. I had a tube down my throat because I couldn't breathe, a tube in my nose because I couldn't eat, and IVs in my arms administering high doses of antibiotics and pain medication. The tube that was down my throat made it impossible for me to fully close my mouth. I was constantly drooling, which would cause me to choke. There were a few things I needed to have beside me on my bed at all times: suction for whatever drool I could gather before it made me cough, a box of tissues for the drool that dripped down my chin and neck, the call button to press if I needed my nurse, and a clipboard with a pen to write down anything I had to say.

The ICU was also disorienting. It was loud and very bright. I heard the sounds of the machines from other rooms and the lights were always on. There was a radio in my room set to the same station 24-hours a day. (I developed PTSD symptoms triggered by the songs I heard. Even years later, when those songs started playing, I felt sick to my stomach and became lightheaded.)

I was still in acute pain from my surgeries and I had contracted pneumonia. Pigtail catheters were inserted into my chest to drain the fluid. Every part of my body felt bruised and beaten.

Soon after arriving in the ICU, I came down with Methicillin-resistant Staphylococcus Aureus (MRSA), a superbug resistant to most antibiotics. It runs rampant in hospitals and can be life-threatening, especially for people who are already ill. Once I was diagnosed, I was put into isolation. The only people allowed to enter my room were my doctors, my nurses, and my husband, and they needed to be double-gowned, gloved, and masked. Once an object was brought into my room, it had to be tossed in the garbage. The medication used to treat the MRSA was a powerful and painful antibiotic administered twice a day through an IV. I dreaded these treatments because it felt like broken glass was being pushed through my veins. If given too quickly, it could cause kidney damage, which meant enduring four hours of this torture every single day.

The psychosis I had experienced in the Step-down Unit intensified while I was in the ICU. I was in a constant state of paranoia and convinced that most of the doctors and nurses were trying to kill me. My delusions told me that I wasn't actually sick and was being kept in the hospital under false pretenses. I believed that I was the victim of a scam that involved extorting money from my family and using my body for experimentation and organ harvesting. It was terrifying. The first time I tried to extubate myself happened when I thought I heard a nurse whisper, "They're trying to kill you, get out!" I tried to leave, but was put in restraints and sedated instead.

I made peace with dying every single night. There were times when I accepted it and thought about my mom, Billy, and my lost son waiting on the other side to greet me and give me the years' worth of hugs I'd missed. But then I thought about my son. My heart ached from the time I was separated from him. I had been in the hospital for over a month and babies change so quickly. I hated that I wasn't with him. The thought of dying and leaving him without a mom was unbearable. In order for me to sleep, I convinced myself that he would be taken care of and that his dad would tell him that his mom loved him very much.

Nate was fantastic throughout my ordeal. He showed up early and was always cheerful. He was very good at compartmentalizing his feelings and approaching things in a practical way. He kept his own charts that monitored everything from my blood pressure to my urine output. It was only when I was out of the hospital that he told me about the awful day my doctors took him into another room and told him that my prognosis wasn't good. They gave me a 50% chance of survival, which had been upgraded from the 25% chance they had given me a few hours earlier. He couldn't imagine telling his son that his mom was never coming home. I felt guilty that I was putting him through these traumatic experiences after six years of marriage. I hated being sick and felt guilty for the people around me who were suffering because of it.

On it went. My days were filled with physical pain from my surgeries, emotional pain from losing one baby, missing the other, and my intense fear brought on by the psychosis. I barely slept during the night. Whenever I started to drift off, the saliva accumulated in my mouth, causing me to choke, bringing a nurse running into my room. She'd placed a catheter into my breathing tube that made me cough more but released the mucus that was clogging my throat. It was horrible and it happened at least three or four times a night.

I dreaded my hair-washing days. They washed it using a bowl of soapy water that was placed at the end of my bed. I lay flat on my back. This was a terrible position for me because it would cause me to cough and I'd need to be suctioned again. One of my nurses decided to put my hair into French braids to keep it from getting tangled between washes. She made it too tight and it hurt, but I didn't have my clipboard and couldn't tell her to stop or be gentler. Without a voice, I couldn't even say, "Ow! Stop!" I felt more vulnerable than ever.

About six weeks into my ordeal, I finally started to make progress. My pneumonia was gone, the MRSA was responding to the antibiotics, and I was getting stronger. It was not what the doctors had expected and I was thrilled to surprise them. But I still had some hurdles to jump. I couldn't leave the ICU until I was off the ventilator. Every morning a doctor performed a flap test, to check my ability to breathe on my own, and every morning I failed. It was heartbreaking. I wanted so badly to see my little boy.

One morning, after I had failed another flap test, I was feeling incredibly disappointed. A nurse with bouncy, blonde hair and a huge smile sashayed into my room and sang, "Good Morning!" I had never met this nurse before and wasn't sure what to expect. She passed the doctor on his way out.

"Did they do the test?" she asked.

I nodded yes.

"And?" she asked hopefully.

I nodded my head no.

"Do you curse?" she asked.

I was confused by her question.

"When you're upset about something," she continued, "Do you curse?"

That made me smile and I nodded a definite yes.

"Okay, then I'll curse for you!"

I cannot express the joy I felt when as my proxy, she gave voice to a beautiful symphony of "Fucks" and "Motherfuckers." It was glorious. She was spectacular and made me feel a little more like myself for the first time in weeks.

I continued to have trouble getting off the ventilator but was told that they were considering giving me a tracheostomy that would allow me to leave the ICU. When I was eleven years old, I had watched an episode of the TV show M*A*S*H, where one of the characters had to perform an emergency tracheostomy in the field using a pen cap instead of a knife. It was incredibly disturbing and creeped me out for years. Yet here I was, eighteen years later, praying that they'd cut a hole in my throat, allowing me to breathe so I could finally get the fuck out of here.

They decided to do the procedure. The respiratory specialist assured me that I would feel a million times better when I was on a regular floor again. I believed him. After it was done, I spent an extra day there making sure everything worked properly before being moved upstairs. Tracheostomies are weird. You go from breathing through your mouth to breathing through a smallish hole in your throat. I still couldn't talk. After a few days, they would try corking the hole by covering it with a plastic flap and asking me to speak. It would be a gradual process.

As my bed was being wheeled out of the ICU and into the elevator, all of my nurses and doctors came to say goodbye. One of my nurses looked at me sweetly and said, "I never want to see you here again!" I agreed with her.

* * *

As soon as the elevator opened on my new floor, I met the two women who would make the rest of my stay much better. Elizabeth was a seasoned pro with ten years of nursing experience. She put me at ease with her self-confidence and compassion. Lindsay, her student, was in charge of my tracheostomy tube. I didn't want a rookie cleaning my throat tube, but she won me over the first time she did it. She was warm and funny and seemed very comfortable with this task. I didn't learn until later that she was absolutely terrified.

"You do realize that you came *this* close to pushing up daisies, right?" Elizabeth said to me. I loved her attitude. She was only a couple of years older than me, but I saw her as a maternal figure. She made me feel safe. I hadn't felt safe in almost two months. Even when she wasn't assigned to me, she came into my room to chat and talk about our sons who were the same age. Lindsay was in her early twenties but looked sixteen. She was spunky and fun, and had a tough, protective side that came out during a visit from a resident and some students he was training. They walked into my room and, without acknowledging me, pulled down my sheet and started examining my incision.

"Hey!" Lindsay yelled at them, "She can't talk, but she can hear and she's a human being! Introduce yourselves!"

They didn't expect to be told off by a student nurse, but to their credit, they did what they were told. I was impressed.

My husband and I didn't talk much about our lost child except to agree on having him cremated. I never knew anyone who had been cremated, but I didn't like the idea of burying him there when we were moving to Toronto.

I still hadn't spoken to my son at home. I'd have to wait until I had made some progress with my tracheostomy and could cap it long enough to have a conversation. The next obstacle I had to face was getting off my feeding tube. Before I could eat on my own, I had to pass the "blue food test." I was presented with a tray that had numerous sections containing different kinds of liquids (water, juice, milk) and creamy foods (yogurt, pudding) that had been dyed blue. The test was to ensure that whatever I ingested would go to my stomach and not my lungs.

I took a sip of the blue water and swallowed it. Then the doctor suctioned out my lungs hoping that the fluid would be clear and not blue. It was clear. It continued to be clear for all of the remaining liquids and foods. The breathing and feeding tubes were removed. I was also off my IV antibiotics and pain medication.

I was recovering quickly and feeling grateful that I would be going home soon. My body was still very weak and would take a few months to fully recover. It was humbling to go from being a fitness instructor who worked out every single day to training my body so I could sit up in a chair, and then stand, and then walk. I learned to be patient with myself.

After a few days, I was ready to make some phone calls. First, my sister. She was elated to hear me speak. When I was ready to call my son, I was afraid he wouldn't remember me. Two months is a long time for a toddler. But he knew his mama. My heart almost exploded when I heard his little voice say, "Mommy," and then the tears came. I missed him so much. I had to wait another week before being discharged. Every day until I left the hospital, I called him and we sang our favorite songs.

The day finally arrived for me to go home. I moved slowly and still had a hole in my throat that would take a couple of days to close on its own, but I was going home. Lindsay and Elizabeth saw me off.

It was time to leave town just four weeks later. The three of us took our lost child's ashes to the beach where we'd spent most of our summer days. I read a poem I had written as we scattered his ashes into the ocean. I felt comforted that my baby was now part of the water and mountains of the west coast, a part of the world that I love.

Our friends had found us a little townhouse to rent in a nice suburb back east. We were all packed up and ready to go. As I sat on the plane waiting for it to take off, I turned to Nate and asked, jokingly, "What else could life throw at us?"

Stupid question.

PART THREE

CASSIDY'S STORY

CHAPTER TWELVE

Not Myself Anymore

"SURPRISE!" the roomful of people shouted as I walked through the door!

"Holy crap!" I yelled back.

We had stopped to visit Nate's family on our way to our new home, and it turned out that they had arranged a surprise party for my thirtieth birthday. I was truly surprised. It had all been cleverly arranged. Most of the guests belonged to my husband's side of the family but I had a small circle of friends and family there, though I immediately noticed my sister's absence. After greeting as many people as I could, I went into the kitchen and called her. Apparently, there had been a misunderstanding leading her to believe that the party had been cancelled. She wouldn't be showing up. I spent the rest of the evening catching up with old friends.

A few days later, my husband left for our new home to unpack and prepare things for us. My recovery was slow but steady. My incisions made it difficult to stand straight and there was still pain when I moved, but I was proud of my progress. I was also proud of my body for all it had overcome. I had spent years judging my body on how it looked while completely ignoring how strong and powerful it was. I promised myself I'd never make that mistake again.

My son enjoyed his time with his adoring grandparents. They were excited to have us back east and closer to them. Barely having any family of my own, I appreciated how loving my in-laws were to their grandson.

The townhouse our friends had found for us was in walking distance from everything we could need. This was very important since I didn't drive. I was more comfortable walking and taking public transportation. My son and I walked everywhere and got to know the neighborhood really well.

Once we were settled in our new life, I started thinking about my father. I hadn't heard from him in years, not even when my mother died, but something in my gut told me to reach out. It wasn't easy, since he had moved out of his apartment and I didn't have his new number, but I eventually tracked him down. I was surprised to learn that he was living in a senior's home. He was only sixty. His diabetes had rendered him blind and in poor health.

"I don't want anything from you," was the first thing out of my mouth when he answered his phone.

I made it clear that I wasn't looking for money and had no interest in rehashing the past. The sole purpose of my call was to tell him that I was back in Toronto and to ask if he needed anything. He told me that he never had any visitors and was lonely. I felt compelled to offer him support. Being sick can be such a scary and isolating experience. We arranged for me to visit him the following week.

We hadn't spoken in years. I felt compassion for him as a human being, but it felt more like a volunteer visiting a stranger than a daughter seeing her father. The first thing I noticed when I walked into his room were the pictures of Lori, Billy, and me hanging on the wall.

We had a nice visit and kept the conversation light. I mentioned my mother briefly. He apologized for not calling when she died and said he felt very sad when he heard the news. He was worried about being rejected if he had tried to reach out. This validated what I had assumed years earlier. He wasn't an evil man . . . he was weak. I told him that I had a son, although I had no plans on introducing them. My father had a habit of disappearing from my life, and while he no longer had the power to hurt me, I needed to protect my son from that kind of disappointment.

That was the only time I went to see him, but we spoke on the phone every week after that. Six months later, he had a heart attack and died.

Losing my father was a much different experience than losing my mother. I had stopped needing my father when I was ten years old. It was still a loss, though. I mourned the loss of something I never really had but had always wanted. I went to his funeral and met relatives I hadn't seen since I was a child. They were gracious to me and seemed appreciative that I showed up. I have no regrets where my father is concerned and, happily, no bitterness towards him.

A couple of months after my father's death, I started yearning for another baby. Most of my doctors back west had cautioned about getting pregnant again: "Why would you risk putting yourself through more trauma?" But Dr. Wen felt differently. He didn't see any medical reason for me not to try and that was good enough for me. After losing one, I knew there was another baby waiting for me. My little boy was going to get the brother I had promised him.

Once again, getting pregnant was easy. Our friends and family were all a bit terrified when we told them the news and I was scared, too. This was my fifth pregnancy and, so far, I'd only brought one child home. But anxious as I was, I was even more excited at the thought of holding another baby.

My first baby loved salt; this one loved chocolate. I gorged on mini chocolate Easter eggs and chocolate covered jellies. I wasn't of big fan of the jellies, but they were my mom's favorite snack and eating them made me feel connected to her.

The pregnancy went smoothly and in the fall, our youngest was born: my second miracle baby. He was fair-haired with a lighter complexion than his brother. He looked just like his mama. It was love at first sight.

My body took a little longer to recover than I thought it would. I really shouldn't have been surprised, since it had been just eighteen months since I had lost a baby and been released from the hospital. But there was something off about how I was feeling. I knew that it wasn't post-partum depression, because I wasn't depressed or angry. It was the opposite. Suddenly I was energized and invincible, despite barely sleeping. It was as though my mind and body were disconnected. I called Dr. Wen in Vancouver and asked his advice.

"Pregnancy impacts your entire body from top to bottom," he said. "It could take a few months before you feel like yourself again."

A few months passed and while I was feeling very connected to and protective of my children, I was feeling less connected to myself. I shared these feelings with Nate. I wish I could say that he told me not to worry and that he had my back during this stressful and confusing time, but that's not how it played out. He wasn't concerned. He saw an opportunity.

One night as we lay in bed, both boys asleep in their rooms, he brought up the subject of a threesome again. I said that I really liked being with *one* person. I've always believed that the more comfortable you are with someone, the more liberated and open-minded you can be sexually. The idea of being with someone new didn't excite me at all.

This time around, unlike the last time he initiated this conversation, he had someone *specifically* in mind.

"What about The Idiot?" he asked.

The Idiot, as I liked to call him, was my least favorite of Nate's friends.

"What *about* The Idiot?" I asked incredulously. Was he really suggesting I have sex with him?

"You know he's always had a thing for you. He thinks you're hot."

"But I just had a baby and I have scars all over my stomach."

"Yes, and he *still* wants to fuck you."

I was sad that when I needed my partner to pull me close, he was pushing me away. But this time I didn't say no. I told him I'd think about it.

He said that would be fine but admitted that he had already talked to Idiot about it, and he was all in. Of course. My husband and his friend were raring to go and waiting for me to join them.

It didn't seem, in the moment, that this would be a turning point in my marriage and my life. All I knew at the time was that I wasn't feeling like myself. I felt a bit crazy. Many years and a lot of therapy later, I would understand the concept of traumatic overload, which happens when someone has been through trauma after trauma without time to heal between, without a chance to process anything. By then, I had certainly experienced more than my share of loss and trauma.

The overload, as one therapist explained to me, can lead to Dissociative Identity Disorder, a mental process which produces a lack of connection in a person's thoughts, feelings, or sense of identity. As I said earlier, it's about self-preservation. It's a coping mechanism. You close off or dissociate your-self from a situation that's too painful for your conscious self to assimilate.

There was no big moment. No revelation. There was no out-of-body experience where Cassidy stood up and strutted out the front door, leaving Marci inert on the couch. I did not feel myself snap and then suddenly, an instant later, I was an entirely different person. The transition was not dra-matic at all. My new persona didn't even have a name yet. She was merely a sense I had of feeling emotionally and psychologically distant from myself. She was my brain's way of protecting me by allowing me to be someone else for a while.

My whole life might have been on shaky ground, but Cassidy made me feel strong, invulnerable, and ready for anything. She would come out whenever I needed her to manage things that were overwhelming, hurtful, or shameful to me. If my husband wanted a sex doll for a wife, Cassidy was game. She wouldn't feel hurt, misused, or degraded. She'd thrive on it.

Nate kept bringing up the threesome with him and The Idiot and, ultimately, I gave in. Marci stepped aside and Cassidy took over. She was flattered to be desired by another man, even one we didn't like very much.

"Okay fine," I told my husband. "Let's do it."

A week later The Idiot came over, and he and my husband made a memory they could laugh about forever. They both enjoyed the experience and wanted more. In my less manic moments, I wasn't feeling tremendously loved. Quite the opposite. But Cassidy convinced me that being lusted after by other men was empowering. It would fill the void. The Idiot kept calling me afterwards, telling me he couldn't stop thinking about me; this fed my ego and alleviated my insecurities. I was surprised at how good it felt to be wanted.

As I said, I was not thinking clearly. I was doing what I felt was neces-sary to survive.

I decided that if I was going to allow myself to be shared in this way, I was going to have to get my body into better shape. My need to be needed opened the door for my eating disorder to storm back into my life. It also gave my husband the chance to play out the fantasies he'd been nursing for years.

CHAPTER THIRTEEN

Cassidy Comes Out

"YOU'VE GOT THE prettiest pussy I've ever seen!" whispered the young dancer in my ear.

This felt like high praise considering the slew of vaginas I imagined she had seen in her line of work.

Nate and I had been to this strip club before. In fact, after our first visit a month earlier, it became our regular Saturday night date spot. I had never been to a strip club before he introduced me to this one and it was pretty much what I was expecting. Loud music pumped through the speakers of a dark room, while men hooted and hollered at women stripping off their clothes.

I wasn't my usual scene, but in Cassidy mode and I loved it.

I was nervous the first time Nate suggested going to a strip club but I was also curious and excited. On our first visit, we sat at a table at the back of the room. We watched the show and took in the atmosphere. After about thirty minutes, he suggested we get a lap dance. We decided that he would choose the dancer and I would approach her to make the deal. I felt like a bit of a badass as the three of us walked to the back room for our private show. It was if I was saying, "I'm confident enough to watch a naked woman dance for my husband!"

As it turned out, I found it awkward. I didn't know where to look. Was I supposed to look at her naked body? Was I supposed to be watching him enjoy the show? It was just weird.

When she was done, I handed her the money and she gave me a hug. As we walked back to our table, my husband admitted to being uncomfortable with me watching. We decided that from then on, he'd do the lap dances on his own and I'd wait at the table. I enjoyed watching the women dance and seeing the reactions they got from the audience.

After a couple of visits, I did more than watch. The dancers at this club made a habit of pulling random women from the crowd onto the stage and getting them to flash their breasts. The night they pointed at me and signaled that it was my turn, I didn't hesitate. The thought of flashing a roomful of strangers was as exhilarating as it was terrifying. With encouragement from the dancers and cheering from the crowd fueling my confidence, I lifted my shirt, unhooked my bra and exposed myself. My husband was thrilled! The rush I felt was addictive.

After that night, the dancers would pull me onstage every time we were there. It wasn't long before the rush wore off and I needed to take things to the next level. That's when I got up on stage and took my clothes off. I was completely naked, in front of strangers. It was exhilarating. My new attitude was, "this is my body and I'll use it however I choose!" I was also seeking Nate's approval. He liked the show but wanted me to push the limits further each time.

I decided there wouldn't be a next time. Cassidy might have been asserting herself but Marci didn't want to do this, and Marci wasn't entirely out of the picture. Nate and I agreed to stop going to the strip club for a while, but the compromise was to continue our adventures in sexual experimentation.

We were having more sex than ever. We were having daily sex at home, and we also made a game of challenging ourselves to have sex whenever we were out without the kids. That included the changing room of an athletics store and multiple restaurant bathrooms. He'd go into the men's room first and when he was alone, he'd signal me to join him. After a quickie, he'd leave first. I'd leave a few seconds later, except when someone would come in and I'd have to wait for them to leave. One night I got stuck in the bathroom stall of a posh wine bar for twenty minutes while men kept walking in and out. My knees started to hurt from standing crouched on the toilet seat. I thought, screw it, and pushed the door open. I gave a wave and smile to the gentleman washing his hands at the sink: "Have a good night!" I don't think there was a restaurant or bar in our suburb that we hadn't christened.

"What's your wildest fantasy?" Nate asked me again in bed one night.

I didn't know how to answer. While I had become more adventurous about showing my body, sharing it with other men was still not of much interest to me. I thought about it some more but I didn't have an answer. It wasn't until I'd been asked the fantasy question for what felt like the millionth time, that Cassidy came up with something.

"Alecia," I said.

"Really?" my husband asked, surprised.

Alecia was the sister-in-law of one of his best friends. I had met her years earlier at a wedding. She hadn't left much of an impression on me but we had recently bumped into her while we were out shopping. She had changed, coming out as a lesbian. Gone was her long, curly hair and pink lipstick. Her new haircut was short and boyish and her face was free of makeup. I couldn't get her off my mind. I was confused by my feelings since I had never been attracted to a woman before.

"So, you want to have sex with Alecia?" he asked.

"I don't know what I want or if she'd even be interested in me. But I'm attracted to her," I said.

Nate was happy that I had finally come up with something that I wanted to do because it allowed him to start planning *his* next fantasy.

"The first step is to find out if she'd have sex with both of us," he said.

"Actually, no," I told him. "This isn't about us. It's about me."

I made it clear that I had zero interest in another threesome. Nate had begged me to share my fantasy and the fact was, my fantasy didn't include him. He wasn't thrilled but agreed to go along with it.

The following week, Alecia's niece was having a birthday party and my kids were invited. We decided that I would take the kids and leave Nate at home. When I got there, she and I started talking right away. I was inexplicably drawn to her and was struggling with how to handle the situation. I made up a lame story about wanting to visit a gay bar for fun. She saw right through me. She asked for my phone number and told me she'd call with some suggestions. She called me the very next day.

"You're attracted to me, aren't you?" she asked.

Before I could answer, she said, "That's okay, I think you're hot as fuck."

My heart was racing. I had no idea what to say. She was unlike anyone I had ever met, and I wanted to get to know her better. She suggested meeting for tea downtown the following day and I agreed. Nate drove me part of the way. *That* was a strange car ride. It was new territory for both of us. I think the lack of control he had over the situation was challenging for him. I kissed him quickly before getting out of the car.

Alecia and I met at a funky coffee shop in the heart of Toronto's gay district. I told her a little bit about my marriage, and she told me about her attraction to straight women. I was mid-sentence when she leaned over the table and kissed me passionately on the lips. I literally felt a shock run through my body.

"Do you wanna get out of here?" she asked.

"Yes," I answered.

We drove around in her car until she found an empty parking lot. Once parked, we unbuckled our seatbelts and lunged at each other. We started kissing and couldn't stop. We made out for three hours. Our connection was intense. I felt like I had known her for years. All I kept thinking about while she drove me home was how weird it should have felt to kiss a woman, but how natural it felt instead. We made plans to get together during the week.

Alicia and I developed a close friendship and saw each other often. The closer we became emotionally, the closer we became physically. We discussed having sex, but my lack of experience with women made me insecure. She told me not to worry and she let me know that she would take the lead the first time we were together. A couple of weeks later, we met at a hotel. Once again, Nate drove me to meet her. Kissing him on the cheek before meeting my soon-to-be lesbian lover was not the sort of thing that I had ever imagined myself doing. Maybe I should have felt guilty about it or concerned about his emotions but the truth was, he seemed totally fine with it and he even shouted a friendly, "Have fun!" as I walked away.

She was already in the room when I got there. I opened the door to find the bed covered in rose petals. She handed me six more and kissed me softly before leading me to the bed. We lay down, held hands, and talked for a bit. She possessed a unique balance of feminine and masculine energies that intoxicated me. She touched my cheek with her hand and told me I was beautiful. She kissed me again. Her lips were the softest I had ever felt. We got lost in each other for hours.

There was something really comforting about being with Alecia that I had never experienced with a man. Instead of worrying about whether my stomach was flat enough or my thighs were lean enough, I just relaxed and enjoyed what was happening. I knew that she had her own insecurities and would not be looking at my body with judgement. There was freedom in that. If I lacked any knowledge about how to please a woman, well . . . Alecia had it in spades. It was an experience I would never forget and one I wanted to repeat. The physical intimacy brought us closer as friends and we continued to spend time together.

At some level, I knew that this was not right. I was a married mother of two children having an intimate relationship with another woman. A lot of people would find that completely unacceptable. But Cassidy could rationalize anything. And it didn't *feel* wrong. My husband was well aware of the situation, so it wasn't as if I was being unfaithful. I trusted Alecia. She had been through her own struggles and was fighting her own demons. She shared things with me that she was unable to share with anyone else. I was as attracted to her vulnerability as I was to her strength.

We continued to have sex when the opportunity presented itself. Before our next encounter, I made sure I did some research so that I wouldn't feel so selfish. Her friendship offered me the love and support I'd been missing from my marriage.

It was around this time that I met Buff Bobby at the gym and started training with him. I started stripping to pay for our sessions. It seemed like a reasonable solution. Marci would take care of the kids during the day and Cassidy would pay for my training and contribute to our household expenses. Somehow the problems of getting adequate sleep and nourishment were brushed aside.

Getting work was not difficult. I called the club we picked, far from our home. I was told which night to show up and to be prepared to jump on stage when called. I could use any music that I wanted except for rap, which was not permitted in the club. When I arrived, I was introduced to the woman in charge. She was in her forties and unfriendly. She introduced me to the DJ and we selected the Britney Spears song I would dance to. I had to be completely naked by the end of the song.

I don't remember feeling anxious about the performance, which was one of the advantages of my manic frame of mind. Once I was done, the manager made a snide comment about my footwear (sandals, it was summer). She told me to buy some proper stripper heels before I came back. I could work as a freelancer. That meant I would not be scheduled. I'd show up when I wanted, and I could keep everything I earned. I just had to tip the DJ. Just like that, Cassidy had a job.

That's not to say there were no tensions. Nate came to see me at work one night and it was a disaster. The other dancers didn't let their partners watch them work because they'd get too jealous. He had the opposite reaction. I was thrilled when I saw him walk into the club and then hugely disappointed when, instead of letting me sit with him, he kept pointing at men he wanted me to dance for.

His attitude around my sexuality troubled and confused me. There were times when he wanted me to act as raunchy and sexy as I could, and other times he'd accuse me of being too sexy. Any time I would mention chatting with a man at a coffee shop, he'd chastise me for being too flirtatious.

"Why are men talking to you?" he asked. "You must be putting out some kind of sexual vibe!"

I found the comment offensive, but maybe he was right? I remember the morning I went to the gym after work. I caught myself climbing on and off a workout bench the same way I'd straddle a customer at the club. I quickly looked around to see if anyone had noticed. It was disturbing. Maybe I wasn't as good at keeping my good girl/bad girl personas separate from each other as I thought.

Alecia and I were still seeing each other, but she had real feelings for me which I found hard to understand. My self-worth was wrapped so tightly around my body that I found it hard to believe anyone could love me for my heart and who I was. Besides, what I needed most was the rush of adrenaline that came from being Cassidy, and she thought love was bullshit. She thought that believing in love made us – made me – weak.

I decided to leave Alecia and hit the stage even harder.

CHAPTER FOURTEEN

Cassidy at the Club

"LICENSE AND REGISTRATION, PLEASE."

The officer impatiently tapped on my car window.

"Shit!" I said under my breath, rolling down my window and reaching into the glove compartment.

"Do you know why I stopped you?" he continued.

I knew exactly why he stopped me. I was speeding. It was unusual for me to be driving so fast. I was normally a cautious driver. On this day, however, I had been listening to a great song on the radio . . . and without realizing it, I'd started driving to the beat of the music.

As soon as I heard the siren and saw the flashing lights behind me, I started to freak out. I had never been stopped by the police before. I also was on my way to my first day shift at the club, so my makeup and outfit all yelled one thing: stripper. Never one to wear a lot of makeup, I had learned how to vamp it up when working. There was nothing subtle about my outfit: skin-tight, camouflage-pattern lycra pants that looked like they'd been painted on, and a matching bra. There was little left to the imagination. I had a change of clothing in my backpack for my drive home, but I hadn't anticipated seeing anyone on the way to the club.

As the officer walked back to his patrol car with my identification, my imagination ran to worst-case scenarios.

"What if he arrests me?"

"What if people find out what I've been doing?"

I could picture the headline in the local newspaper, "Suburban Stripper Mom Stopped for Speeding!"

He simply returned to my car with my I.D. and a ticket and told me to be more careful before sending me on my way.

I got to the club, handed my song selections to the DJ and hit the floor running. The speed trap had cut into my dancing time, leaving me with less than three hours to work before having to pick my kids up from school.

"Watch out for the religious dudes," one of the dancers warned me as the first customers started walking in.

"Pardon?"

"Day shifts are full of religious dudes who sneak away from their respectable jobs to come here and stick their fingers inside whichever dancer is available. It's gross!"

I had not expected that I'd be spending my afternoon protecting my vagina from penetration by the filthy fingers of complete strangers. The problem was, it was slim pickings at that hour. There were three dancers working and few customers to approach.

After performing my first stage set of the day, I was waved over by a group of the men that I had been warned about. I braced myself for the worst and that's exactly what I got. I had barely started my lap dance when I felt a hand reach into my G-string! I jumped back and yelled, "No!" With a creepy smile, he said, "Just a little?"

Fuck that. I stormed away from the table. One of the bouncers saw what had happened and warned the men that they'd be kicked out if it happened again. It was a nice gesture, but meaningless. I was not going back. Yes, I was willingly naked for strangers, but there were limits. I wasn't about to be violated.

This wasn't the first time one of my customers ignored the club's "Do not touch" policy. A few nights earlier, around closing time, I was dancing for my last customer of the evening. He was a clean-cut gentleman in his late thirties. I had just started the second of the two lap dances he had requested when he grabbed my hand and placed it on his crotch.

I didn't want to cause a scene. I calmly took my hand away while giving him a "don't be a naughty boy" look and kept dancing. Once again, he took my hand and placed it on his bulge. I stopped dancing and reminded him that what he wanted was against the rules. He smiled. "Come on," he said. "I'll give you an extra $40."

I hate to admit it but part of me was tempted. We were on the second level of the club where it was darker and a little more private. I was already rubbing my naked body against him. Would one step further really be so horrible? I decided that it would be.

"Can't do it. Sorry," I told him.

He was not deterred. Once again, he took my hand. This time his pants were unzipped and his penis was front and center. I had two choices: call for a bouncer and have the guy kicked out, or stay quiet and get through the last few seconds of the song. I really didn't want to make a huge scene and was worried that if he got tossed from the club, I wouldn't get paid. I chose to stay quiet, get my money, and go home.

Unfortunately, it wasn't so easy. As soon as the song ended and the lights were turned on, I was approached by a bouncer and one of the dancers. She looked pissed.

"She was jerking him off!" the girl yelled at the bouncer while pointing at me.

Holy crap. I really hadn't. I had thought about it for a split second, but hadn't gone through with it.

"We don't do that kind of thing here!" she continued shouting, "You're making us all look bad!"

So much for not making a scene. I assured her that while the customer wanted a hand job, I had repeatedly turned him down.

She didn't believe me. While she was yelling, my customer had an innocent look on his face that said, "Who me?" I felt sick to my stomach. I thought I was either going to get kicked out of the club for solicitation or the irate dancer was going to beat the crap out of me. Possibly both.

After what felt like forever, the customer was told to leave and I was given a stern warning that if I was ever caught doing what I had been accused of, I'd be in big trouble.

On my drive home that night, all I kept thinking was, "How is this my life now?"

I shouldn't have been surprised that it happened. I suppose it's natural for a man to want to touch the naked woman who is gyrating against him, but there were other clubs for that. One of the reasons I chose to work at this one was the fact that they obeyed the law. Many strip clubs did not. One night, Nate had taken me to a different club to test it out. When I got there, I was taken down a long hallway lined with tiny cubicles with curtains as doors. It was explained to me that they were the V.I.P. rooms. In these rooms, customers got to spend private time with the dancer or dancers of their choice. Price was to be agreed upon by the people involved as well as the services being provided. This was enough for me to know I didn't want to work there.

I was lucky to work at my club. Sex workers deserve as much respect as anybody else. Not all women in the business have that luxury, however. They can be treated like property, rented out for a few bucks at a time. Even at my club, there were times when I felt like that. The wrong customer can make you feel like trash with one unkind word or misplaced hand. I tried not to let them affect me too much and to stand my ground, which meant that I refused to put up with Mr. Filthy Fingers on my day shift.

I didn't make much money that day. I spent most of my time with a young man who was too sweet and naïve to be spending his lunch hour at a strip club. He looked to be about twenty-five and lonely. I was happy to sit with him and dance for him, but after a while I got the impression that he was looking for a girlfriend. He kept saying how much he liked me and how I seemed different from the other girls. He asked for my number and my work schedule. I gave him neither and explained that I was not what he was looking for. He said he disagreed but would respect what I was saying.

After spending a significant amount of time at his table, I told the young man that I was required to dance on stage before leaving for the day. He thanked me for my time and attention.

Being on stage was my favorite part. I found it fun. I was never able to master the pole the way some of the other dancers had. It's much harder than it looks. I was a decent dancer and actually enjoyed performing so what I lacked in pole skills, I tried to make up in showmanship. Sassy Cassy!

I left the club that day with barely enough money to cover my speeding ticket. I also left with the feeling that maybe it was time to stop dancing. As much as I liked making my own money, stripping was starting to feel less empowering. I gave myself a week to decide.

Meanwhile, Nate had been spending his free time on the internet planning our next sexcapade. We were off to our first swingers' event.

CHAPTER FIFTEEN

Cassidy Swings

"I FEEL LIKE WE'RE AT a Bar Mitzvah," I whispered to my husband as we walked into the party.

It was our first swingers' event. He had heard about it online, and it was not what I was expecting. My imagination had me envisioning hot, young couples wearing matching leather g- strings, sipping exotic cocktails in a room with red velvet walls. I'm not sure where I got that idea from, but the reality was simply a small group of middle-aged couples dancing to '90s music in the party room of an economy hotel. Hubby got himself a rye-and-ginger from the bar, and we chose a table to sit at. A few couples smiled at us from the dancefloor, but we pretty much kept to ourselves until Belinda and Daniel approached.

"Well hello, newbies!" Belinda said.

"Welcome to the jungle!" added Daniel.

I liked them. Their friendly energy put me at ease. Belinda said they spotted us as first-timers as soon as we walked in.

"Don't worry, newbies!" she assured us, "We'll teach you everything you need to know."

We spent the rest of the night getting to know each other. Belinda fancied herself a swingers' whisperer. Daniel told us they'd been in the swinging lifestyle for several years. He said it added a little spice to their relationship. They had recently become involved in the online sex industry, turning a guestroom in their home into a small studio kitted out with computer equipment, professional lighting, and a bed. In front of the bed was a chest filled with an assortment of sex toys.

According to Belinda, it was the easiest money she'd ever made. Men would contact her through an internet group advertising virtual, interactive sexual experiences with hot girls (this was in the early 2000s, and the whole online scene was not as advanced as it is now). Once they'd connected online and paid the fee, the men would call her on the phone to make their requests. They'd tell her where to touch herself, how to touch herself, and in what position to be in when she touched herself. The longer she performed, the more money she made. She said it was a lot better than folding clothes at The Gap.

We made plans to meet Daniel and Belinda the following weekend for dinner followed by sex. We chose a restaurant and hotel in a neutral location. I felt very strange for the entire week leading up to our meeting. While Daniel seemed to be a likeable guy, I barely knew him and had agreed to have sex with him. The fact that my husband, who was very excited about it, would be in the next bed having sex with Daniel's wife made it even weirder. I couldn't blame him for being excited: Belinda had not been subtle about how much she liked him and wanted him. It was odd to see a woman openly flirting with my husband, but I didn't feel jealous about it.

By that point, most of the feelings I'd had for my marriage had evaporated. Our relationship had changed monumentally since I was in the hospital. My husband no longer saw me as his wife to be protected but as a toy to be shared. Maybe I should have tried harder to avoid the sharing or find other ways to fulfil his fantasies, but I lost the battle. It was devastating, another blow to my self-esteem. By now I knew how to respond, however. More Cassidy. I would find power and a sense of control in the attention that my sexuality was attracting.

A few days before our date, Belinda emailed me a list of rules. These were the unspoken but universally understood rules of most swinging clubs.

Rule 1. No single men.
Single women were always welcome, but no club was open to single dudes trying to hook up with married women.

Rule 2. Women are in control.
Initial contact is made between the wives/girlfriends. Men never approach the women.

Rule 3. No means No.
If a couple is approached to dance or chat and they aren't interested, there is no further conversation about it.

Rule 4. Always practice Safe Sex.

Rule 5. Communication is key.
Talk to your partner before, during, and after. You need to regularly check in with each other and make sure you're both on the same page. If one wants to leave, you both leave.

Rule 6. Swing to enhance a marriage, not save it.
The biggest mistake a struggling couple can make is to involve other people in their relationship. A relationship has to be solid for this type of lifestyle to work successfully.

The big night arrived, and Nate and I met our new friends for a little dinner and debauchery. The hotel we went to had two double beds. Belinda and my husband took one and Daniel and I the other. My husband and Belinda had sex. I know they did. I was there and I saw it happening, yet I don't remember a single feeling I had about it. I watched them get naked and engage in all kinds of sexual activity, but I felt nothing.

My first swinging experience was a lot less exciting than my husband's. While he was getting laid, I had to listen to Daniel assure me that his inability to sustain an erection had nothing to do with me. He said it was common for men in the swinging lifestyle to suffer from performance anxiety. Apparently having sex in front of their wives made them uncomfortable. I wasn't sure if it was an issue for "a lot" of men or just Daniel, and I didn't care. I was bored. As soon as Nate was done, we left.

My husband found another swingers' club for us to try out. This club was closer to what I had imagined. The lights were low, the music was loud, and the women showed more cleavage, and more cheek, beneath barely-there lingerie. Most of the men were dressed in pants and dress shirts. I had chosen to wear one of Cassidy's favorites, a black negligee from the strip club. I felt like a teenager when I covered my outfit in baggy pants and a sweater to greet our babysitter and leave my kids with a goodnight kiss.

After standing by the bar for fifteen minutes, we noticed a group of people sitting at a table by the dancefloor who were signaling us to join them. As we walked over, we could feel their eyes burn into us.

"Fresh meat, huh?" said one of the husbands. Once again, we were immediately spotted as newcomers, adding to our allure. It was clear that the two in the middle were the power couple of the club. He was a plastic surgeon and she was a stay-at-home mom to their three teenagers. She had clearly benefitted from his skills. She was the closest thing to a living Barbie that I had ever seen. Barbie was as quiet as her husband, Ken, was gregarious.

"Join us!" he shouted, signaling to one of the men to give up his chair for me. We sat and he introduced us to his friends. There were five couples, all attractive, all in their forties. We were in our early thirties, so we weren't just fresh meat, we were young, too. I learned that many of the couples had started swinging as a way for the wives to experience other women. It was a safe environment for them to act out fantasies while their husbands watched. I got felt up by a lot of women that night. I was fine with it, but it did not turn me on. It was more stimulating for my husband to watch than for me to experience. My friendship with Alecia taught me that I wasn't attracted to women in general—I was attracted to *her*. That said, it wasn't as if I was repulsed at the idea of being intimate with a woman. It just wasn't my preference.

After a few hours, Ken invited us to join him, Barbie, and two of the other couples at a motel nearby. While we had not planned on participating in an orgy that night, we took a when-in-Rome attitude and agreed to go along.

It was a bizarre experience. Four couples in one bed. All I remember was the feeling of numerous hands touching my body and not being quite sure who they belonged to. I also remember one of the husbands sitting off to the side looking miserable. He and his wife had got involved because of her interest in women.

I made out with a bunch of people. I'm pretty sure I had sex with two men and one woman. I don't know who or what my husband did while we were there and we never discussed it.

After that night, we jumped into the whole swinging thing. The following Saturday, after dancing and socializing at the club, Ken and Barbie invited us back to their place. They lived in a mansion in one of the wealthiest neighborhoods of Toronto. I didn't see very much of it. We were ushered in through a side door and taken directly to a guest bedroom. The four of us climbed onto the bed and started messing around. As always, I found the sex itself unsatisfying but was excited by how rebellious it made me feel. Ken and Barbie had been part of the swinging scene for years and their relationship really impressed me. Barbie told me that no matter how tired they were at the end of a night spent with another couple, they ended the evening by having sex with each other. They put their relationship above everything else. That kind of connection was strangely sweet and made me a little envious.

During one of our nights at the club, Nate surprised me by letting me choose a couple to approach. Up until then, he had done all the choosing for both of us, but for whatever reasons, this night was different. The tall, broad, bald-headed man with the goatee was the first man I had found attractive since we started swinging. I was excited to meet him and his wife. As per club rules, I introduced myself to her first and then, with her permission, waved my husband over.

She was a petite brunette and he was a police officer. He was anxious about destroying his reputation by being seen at a club like this. It was only their second visit, which made them fresher meat than we were. They hadn't yet decided if the lifestyle suited them and wanted to have one experience under their belts before they made their decision. We hung out together that night and then arranged to meet for a date the following week.

Unfortunately, our experience with these newbies ended up being reminiscent of my first experience. Nate was getting laid while I was discussing how common it was for men to have trouble performing. I wasn't terribly surprised that the policeman couldn't get it up. He was worried about his job, and he had never seen his wife doing naughty things with another man. He was not enjoying it. We were their first couple and their last.

Another of the couples we met at the club invited us to a house party some friends of theirs were throwing. We accepted the invitation. It was like walking onto a porn set. Each room had a theme. There was a BDSM room that was equipped with masks, whips, and other similar paraphernalia. Another room with bear skin rugs, fur covered handcuffs, and a sex swing. I found the room with the glory holes a little disturbing. There were rooms for group play and for one-on-one action. Nate and I stumbled into a room with a king-sized bed and were encouraged to have sex with each other while strangers watched. It was strictly voyeuristic, so no one was allowed to join in. At that point, having sex with each other, even in front of an audience, seemed pretty tame. We climbed on to the bed, got naked and had sex while people were casually walking in and out, some staying for the entire show.

On paper, swinging suited us. Or, rather, this lifestyle suited Cassidy and my husband. Our strong sex drives were being serviced and the fact that we were doing it together was supposed to keep things open and honest. It *seemed* like it would be a good fit for us, but my need to be loved and my Nate's need for control made it a disaster waiting to happen.

When I was not in a manic state, when I had time to stop and think, I felt like I was losing my mind. Between the humiliating threesomes, the sex in public places, the stripping, the swinging, and the lack of sleep, the sexual side of me had gotten completely out of control.

I had a hard time accounting for myself. I was in my thirties and all I wanted to do was act out. I was mad at Nate over the state of our marriage and the way he made me feel, mad at God for taking away my family, mad at society for its indifference, and mad at myself for being weak and defenseless.

I wish more than anything that my need to rebel would have taken me out of the situation I was in and maybe even out of my marriage. Instead, it took me further into chaos. I wish I could have understood that my value as a human being was not dependent on how fuckable men found me to be. But the more vulnerable I felt, the more Cassidy came to the forefront.

I've often wondered my rebellion or acting out, or whatever we call it, took the form of a double life of sexual adventure. The first part is not hard to explain. Double lives came naturally to me. Almost all of the men in my life had coped with their needs by splitting off into some sort of a double life. I had many examples to choose from.

That I would take refuge in sex rather than drugs, alcohol, gambling, or one of the other many forms of addiction—or instead of violence or religion—was probably rooted in my earlier experience. When Billy died, I had tried to assert control over my life by deliberately losing my virginity. I was a teenager back then, and I didn't have a lot of other cards to play. Even as an adult, however, it still seemed as though using my body to prove my desirability and control my destiny was my best option. We use what we have, and I didn't feel as though I had any other options.

I've since come to see that my sexual escapades and my eating disorder were closely related. My self-worth was entirely wrapped up in how I looked and whether or not other people thought I was attractive. Sex and eating (or, rather, not eating) were ways to assert control and make myself attractive. They were also ways of dealing with my sense of vulnerability and my deep insecurities. There was a strange logic to it. If I was going to have sex, I needed to be skinny. And I had to have sex because if I stopped, I'd overeat and gain weight. The answer, obviously, was to have as much sex as I could and to be as skinny as possible.

I started seeing every man as a possible conquest. I could be at the gas station, supermarket, or even sitting in my car at a red light, and I'd be sizing up the men around me. "Could I have sex with him?" I'd ask myself a dozen times a day about random strangers who crossed my path. After years of feeling like I could never be pretty enough, I was feeling sexy and lusted after, like a femme fatale from an old movie. It was intoxicating and addictive. Of course, like all addictions, the highs were no match for the feelings of shame and regret that followed.

One night, I ended up in Buff Bobby's bed after having told my husband

I was going out with a girlfriend. That's when I knew it was time to reach out for help.

With my mind consumed with thoughts of sex, I looked up the number of a Sex Anonymous group in my area. I wasn't sure if I had an actual sex addiction, but I wasn't comfortable with how easily I was allowing my body to be used. The conversation I had with the moderator of the group was interesting. He didn't sound thrilled at the idea of me showing up and made me aware of three facts:

1. I would be the only woman in the group.
2. I would not be allowed to wear makeup and my hair would have to be pulled back.
3. I was not allowed to curse.

As soon as I heard that, my first thought was, "Oh no. I'll be the only woman in a group of sex addicts. That sounds unsafe." Followed quickly by my second thought: "Oh wow. I'll be the only woman in a room of sex addicts. That sounds cool." I was imagining the attention I would receive walking into a roomful of men who couldn't control their overactive sex drives. I would have felt like a fucking goddess. It was tempting. Fortunately, deep down, I knew that it would be cruel to take advantage of someone else's addiction to satisfy my own. The fact that I would have to abstain from sex for a year was also a huge deterrent. I was going to have to manage my sexual impulses on my own. I stopped stripping for several months.

Nate was not helpful.

"Hey, remember what Belinda told us about making extra money on the internet?" he asked me after dinner one night.

"Yeah, what about it?"

"You should do that!"

He missed the financial contributions from my stripping career. He figured I could give the online sex industry a shot. After all, both kids were in pre-school a few days a week. I had the time. I had no idea what I would have to do to become an online sex worker but my husband had done some research. He found a website where I could sign up, post my picture, and make myself available for sex shows. Feeling a bit guilty about not being able to contribute to our household expenses, and not yet having my sexual impulses under control, I agreed to it.

This didn't go well. First of all, Belinda and Daniel had done it properly. They knew that in order to make money, they'd have to invest in the proper equipment. Nate didn't want to spend any money, leaving me with very little to offer prospective customers. There would be no way for them to speak to me or hear me. All we had was a crappy camera. The men would only be able to type their requests and watch me do things to myself. They could actually directly interact with the other women on the site. That made my offerings less attractive. I promised to give it a shot anyway.

It was one of the most degrading, demoralizing experiences of my life. After dropping my kids off at pre-school, I sat on a stool in my basement wearing a bra and panties, waiting for someone to pay to see me. The basement was completely unfinished, with concrete floors, exposed wood ceilings, a washer and dryer. I sat there for hours. This was the early 2000s so there were no apps on my cell phone that would let me kill time by listening to music or watching TV. I just sat there, waiting. A few men contacted me and complained about how cheap our set-up was. When it was time for me to pick up my kids, I got dressed and promised myself I would never do that again.

I walked down the hallway of the daycare facility feeling like an alien. I looked at all of the other moms picking up kids. There were the professional working moms and the stay-at-home moms. And me, the mom who had just spent the day trying to sell sex online. Unsuccessfully.

Looking at the kids around me, I thought of myself at their age. Never in a million years would I have imagined that things would turn out as they had. I was supposed to become a successful actress, not a failed porn star. I could only assume that the confident, goal-oriented girl I used to be would be incredibly disappointed to learn what I was doing now. Yes, the internet sex was my husband's idea, but I could have said no. He didn't lock me in the basement. I agreed to it.

I was beating myself up in this way before I finally found my boys. Seeing their faces light up when they saw me at their classroom doors was always the best part of my day. Nothing cheered me up faster than tight hugs and loving kisses from my kids. On the drive home we sang along to the radio and chatted about their day. When Nate got home, I let him know what a disaster our new business turned out to be. I told him that I would not be doing it again.

"You do realize you have to stay down there all day, right?" he asked. "It takes time to build a client base."

I realize now that he must have been detached from our relationship. At the time, I thought he was just good at compartmentalizing Marci, who read bedtime stories to our kids, and Cassidy, his sexual playmate. For me, the lines were blurred and my self-esteem was suffering. If he wanted more cash, he was going to have to make it himself.

It would have been nice if that humiliation had served as a wake-up call . . . but all it did was make me feel like an unattractive failure. I doubled down on my eating disorder. Even if I was no longer for sale in my own basement, my self-esteem still required me to feel sexy and to have sex, so that was it for food.

I gave up eating solids. I found the lowest calorie shake I could find and drank just enough of it to get me through my killer gym workouts. I lost a ton of weight. My neighbors were starting to worry about me and asked my husband if I was seriously ill. Whenever I'd go to a restaurant with my kids, they'd ask, "Are you eating today, Mommy, or just watching?" On a trip to the amusement park, my son pointed to my back and shouted, "Look! Mommy's a dinosaur!" He'd noticed how sharply the bones of my spine stuck out from my bikini top.

This body that I fought so hard to keep alive just a few years earlier deserved to be cherished and protected. Instead, it was being used and starved and taken for granted. I knew this was happening but I felt powerless to do anything to change it. The hunger that I felt for food was nothing compared to how starved I was for the attention of others. It didn't matter where it came from or who was offering it. If men showed an interest, my body was theirs to borrow, even if those men were married.

PART FOUR

THE LONG WAY HOME

CHAPTER SIXTEEN

The Reckoning

HOLY. FUCKING. SHIT.

It was 4:00 a.m. My plan, as always, was to take a quick look at my emails before heading to the gym for a two-hour workout. Instead, I was staring at my computer screen, paralyzed with panic.

There were three new emails in my inbox. I didn't have the courage to read them but I had a pretty good idea of what to expect from the subject lines.

First: YOU FUCKING BITCH!

Second: Are you sleeping with my husband?

Third: She knows . . .

Yep. These emails were all about the married men I'd been sleeping with since my own marriage went off the rails: Fireman, School Dad, and Home-Towner. In the first two cases, their wives were writing to me so that they could accuse me – or just curse me out. In the last case, the Home-Towner wanted to warn me that his wife had found out about us.

I felt sick. "Take a deep breath," I told myself, but my heart was pounding so fast that the only breaths I could muster were short and quick. My chest hurt and I started to feel lightheaded. I wondered if this was what a heart attack felt like. I could see the coroner's report: death by adultery. Who would mourn me?

I was in the basement of our townhouse. My husband and our kids were sound asleep in their bedrooms upstairs. I felt incredibly alone . . . although even if I had been lying beside my husband, I'd still have felt alone.

I didn't want to read the emails but I reminded myself: "You did this to yourself."

I clicked on the message from Fireman's wife, and braced for the first of three ass-kickings that I would receive.

How can you live with yourself? I found your disgusting emails! He's a married man with three kids! Don't you even care about that? You must have no morals! Who raised you? They must be so ashamed of you! Leave my husband alone or I'll ruin your life!

Harsh, but not undeserved. I did have sex with her husband. Does it help at all that I didn't enjoy it? Does the fact that I hated myself for doing it make it any less despicable? Probably not.

I'd met Fireman on a trip to my local fire station with my kids. A few years ago, I'd decided that on the birthdays of my brother and mother, instead of mourning their deaths, I would go celebrate their lives by performing random acts of kindness around the city. I would pop into a coffee shop and anonymously treat ten strangers to their morning coffees, or I'd pay for the car behind me in the McDonald's drive-thru. I knew my family would love me remembering them that way.

About a month earlier, on my mom's birthday, I'd baked cookies and taken them, along with my boys, to the fire station in our neighborhood. We were greeted by Fireman and a younger firefighter who let my boys sit in a firetruck and play with the siren. On our way out, Fireman asked me for my name, phone number, and email address, so the station could send me a thank you note. That night, I got an email from him. He thanked me for the cookies and told me how attractive he thought I was, and how nice it would be if we could stay in touch.

"Uh oh," I thought when I read his message. I had little interest in staying in contact with him but, to be honest, I was desperate for any kind of attention. I know how pathetic that must sound, but at that point even misplaced and misguided attention was better than none at all. "Thanks and sure!" I wrote.

He continued to send me friendly emails for the next couple of days, during which time I learned that he was an unhappily married (aren't they all?) father of three. I should have stopped speaking to him. My own marriage might have been a shit show, but I had no business interfering in anybody else's. Instead, after a few more email conversations, we arranged to meet.

He came to my house. I was alone and had a few hours before picking my kids up from school. We had sex. I barely remember it. I was becoming increasingly alienated from my body, so much so that all the sex I had in those days was like an out of body experience. I was there, but also not.

I had no idea how to respond to Fireman's wife. I tried to be honest:

I'm sorry.

I don't know what else to say except that you're right. I am a disgusting person and my parents would be ashamed of me, if they weren't already dead. I realize that there's nothing I can say to make things better. I'm just very, very sorry. I haven't spoken to him in a few weeks and I promise that I will never speak to him again. Sorry.

Two more to go.

How did I get myself in this situation? I didn't think of myself as a cheater. My father was a cheater and I never understood how anybody could cheat on their partner. I thought back to the time when Nate and I were in Vancouver and I was working at the café. When that customer had asked me out, a little part of me was tempted and I felt horribly guilty about it. I politely declined and then went home and immediately told my husband about it. I wanted him to get me back on track. I hated being even a little tempted. I was not going to cheat.

But here I was, a woman who wanted never to cheat, having to apologize for screwing three different married men. Cassidy, as usual, had her rationalizations. I was not a cheater: my husband had forfeited my fidelity. By pressuring me to have sex with other people, he hadn't just blurred the lines of our relationship, he'd completely erased them. But Marci wasn't buying it. If I wasn't a cheater, I was an accomplice to cheating, a jezebel, the other woman, and that felt shitty enough.

Next up, School Dad:

> *Hi,*
>
> *I'm School Dad's wife. I'm sorry to be contacting you, but your name came up in my husband's contacts, along with several other women and I'm reaching out to all of you to see what I can find out. I know he's screwing around; I just don't know who with. This isn't the first time he's cheated and I should have done something about this years ago, but I didn't. I know you've emailed each other but I don't know the nature of your relationship. Is there anything you can tell me?*

There were a lot of things I could have told her. That he had approached me at a coffee shop near our kids' school and started chatting with me and how, after bumping into each other a few more times, we'd exchanged contact information and eventually ended up meeting for sex.

I *could* have told her that, but I was not going to. She knew he was cheating and apparently with a few different women. She didn't need to know the details. I did admit to engaging in inappropriate emails with him and apologized for that much. I was pretty sure she was just looking to validate her suspicions and I gave her that. But I'm also a coward because I was terrified that if she did know the details, it would get around the school and my kids would find out. Despite the insanity around me, I thought about my sons constantly and I was terrified of doing something that would hurt them.

I hoped this meant School Dad would stop calling me. My interactions with him were particularly demoralizing. My neediness and loneliness had turned me into an easy lay and he was just using me to get whatever he was not getting at home. He and I played a little game: he pretended to feel like there was a special connection between us and I pretended not to know he was full of shit. I let him have what he wanted because for the twenty minutes that we were together, I felt a false sense of control over my body, as if it was my choice to have sex with him. But the feeling was always short-lived and followed by a deep sense of shame. When he left, I would binge on junk food until I hurt.

Sometimes I told myself I was using sex with School Dad as a way of punishing myself for the sex I was having with everybody else. I realize that makes no sense, but my life had stopped making sense long before this. Fucking him and eating until I hurt were how I expressed to myself that I hated what I was doing. But I couldn't stop and I had no one to turn to with problems like this. My only source of support was Nate, and he was enjoying my trauma-induced behavior too much to help me escape it.

In my heart, I don't believe that my husband was actively trying to hurt me, but I think that he knew what was going on and how he made me feel, and he kept doing it anyway. I was engaging in behaviors that would never have crossed my mind if he had not encouraged them. I had my own problems—the eating disorder, my body issues, my losses and traumas—and I was heartbroken that my husband wanted to share my body with other men. Instead of holding me close to protect me, he was throwing me to the wolves so he could watch them devour me.

But I can't lay it all on him. In my cold, sober moments, like when I was faced with these three emails, there were no excuses. It didn't matter who pushed me. It didn't matter what I'd experienced, or how unhinged I'd been, or why. At the end of the day, we're all answerable for our own behavior, and sleeping with married men is a shame for which I will never forgive myself. I closed my eyes and took a deep breath before opening email number three, from Home-Towner himself:

> *She knows.*
> *I accidentally left some of our emails on the computer and some of our texts on my phone. I'm sorry. She knows it's you. I don't think she'll say anything to your husband. I can't contact you again for a few days.*
> *Sorry again.*

First, how hard would it have been to delete an email, moron? Second, I'm a horrible person. There were three women feeling shitty that morning and I was the reason why. I felt sick and incredibly sorry that I had caused so much damage.

Home-Towner was a guy who I knew back from when I was a teenager in Montreal. We didn't know each other well, just through mutual friends. Then we'd bumped into each other at a coffee shop in my neighborhood. He didn't live in the area, but I noticed that after we bumped into each other the first time, he came in regularly. We became friends and then, one day, at the coffee shop, he said, "I find myself thinking about you all the time, even though I know I shouldn't."

Once again, my response should have been, "You're right! You shouldn't be thinking about me, and definitely not telling me if you are. You're married. I'm married. This is where it ends."

Of course, that's not where it ended. If it had, I'd only have had two gut-wrenching emails to deal with.

We both wanted something from each other. I wanted to feel needed, and he wanted a shiny, new toy. He'd married his high school sweetheart and never said a single negative word about her to me. According to him, she was a great wife and mother to their kids. He said that he loved her very much but found himself drawn to me because there was something special about me.

Eye roll. The only reason he was drawn to me was because I was not the one and only woman he'd been sleeping with since he was eighteen. I wasn't special. I just wasn't her. I knew it and he knew it, but again, we pretended we have a deep connection that we couldn't deny. We got on with it.

Home-Towner and I didn't actually have sex, but we did fool around and that was bad enough. We also became friends. When I found out that I needed to have liver surgery, he was the first person I called, even before my husband. Somehow, sharing these personal feelings with him seemed more of betrayal than fooling around.

His email meant I was losing a friend. It sucked, but what his wife had to deal with was so much worse. She is a good person who would never do the things I'd done. I was the whore. I wished I could have apologized to her directly, but is that ever how it works? Could I just call her up and say, "Hey, Mrs. Home-Towner, sorry for being such a big ol' slut and messing around with your life partner" . . .?

I felt overwhelmed. One email would be bad. But three emails in one day about three different men? I could hardly breathe. I was drenched in guilt and shame and I knew it had to stop and it had to stop now. I wanted to be able to look at myself in the mirror without feelings of disgust and revulsion.

I had to tell Nate. I had to tell him what had been going on so he'd understand we needed to get our marriage back on track, if that was even possible. We couldn't keep tossing my body around like I was worthless. It was killing my self-esteem and my self-worth. It was harmful to other people. I also had two babies to raise and I needed to be emotionally and physically healthy enough to do it.

I felt the tears starting to flow and I couldn't stop shaking as I walked up the stairs to confront my husband. I knew he wouldn't be shocked. I mean, we shared the same email account. He probably knew at least some of what had been going on, but hearing about it would be upsetting for him. I was not sure if he'd be more hurt or angry. I didn't know how he'd feel about the fact that I'd crossed whatever boundaries he thought remained in our marriage.

I crawled into bed, sobbing uncontrollably. He heard me and rolled over. "What did you do?" he asked in a tone that sounded a little annoyed.

I told him everything. I was waiting for him to yell at me or, more likely, lecture me on all of the ways that I'd fucked up. Instead, he paused for a second and said, "If you let me fuck you any way I want, I'll forgive you."

No anger. No lecture. No love. I rolled over and got ready to apologize.

CHAPTER SEVENTEEN

Admitting Madness

WHILE AGREEING TO ENGAGE IN taboo sex was enough to earn my husband's forgiveness – for what that was worth – I realized that forgiving myself wouldn't be as easy. I was a slut for screwing around with married men, a bitch for not being a better wife, and a failure for putting my family in such jeopardy. Reading emails from those wives was the shock that I needed to wake me from three-years of sleepwalking as Cassidy.

I left two messages for my therapist begging him to call me back. When we finally spoke, his instructions were simple. Stop it. Stop all of it.

No more visits to strip clubs. No more swingers' parties. No sex except with my husband, in our home. I needed to reconnect to the parts of me that had nothing to do with sex. My husband seemed fine with this at first, but just a few days later surprised me by suggesting we return to the swingers' club.

"I told you that I can't do that again!" I said. "It's damaging to my physical and emotional well-being, not to mention our marriage."

"What if we just watch?" he asked.

I explained to him that just watching would still be subjecting me to behavior that was eating away at my self-worth and eroding our relationship. He was clearly disappointed but eventually accepted the boundary I was setting.

Reigning in my sexual activity was challenging but not nearly as tough as managing my eating disorder. Again, they were related – both rooted in that need to be attractive and in control – but the eating disorder went deeper and it had been there longer. It was vicious and relentless. I knew I would need to get it under control if I stood a chance at being healthy again, but it wasn't until after the three emails and speaking to my therapist that I began to appreciate just how berserk my diet and exercise had become.

On most days, I was the only person working out at my gym between the hours of 2 a.m. and 5 a.m. When the kid working at the reception desk would ask me why I trained in the middle of the night, I told him that I worked odd hours, leaving me with no other options. The reality was that I equated rest with laziness.

It had started during my stripper days. I would forgo sleep completely on the nights that I worked, so I could jump back into my role as mom as soon as I got home. I'd have breakfast ready when both kids woke up and their plans set for the day. My boys have always been very active, and loved spending time at the playground or at one of the many kids' activity centers in our neighborhood.

My overly-restrictive diet and lack of sleep should have left me feeling exhausted, as if I was running on fumes. Instead, I felt the opposite. It was as if my body didn't know it was supposed to be tired. The madness wouldn't allow it.

One Sunday at midnight, I left our house and walked instead of driving the 8.5 km to the gym. After eating more than I had planned at dinner, I felt compelled to immediately work off the calories. The walk was unnerving, but the return after completing a two-hour workout was terrifying. At 4:00 a.m. the streets were eerily quiet, except for the sound of the occasional car driving by. I chose not to listen to music through my headphones so I could hear the footsteps of anyone who may have tried to run up behind me.

The one thought that kept running through my mind was, "What will my husband tell my boys if I get murdered tonight? How will he explain why their mom was out by herself in the middle of the night?"

There would have been no explanation that made sense. I'm ashamed to admit that as afraid as I was of being attacked, I was more afraid of gaining weight. I felt selfish, and that selfishness translated into still more guilt.

Once I'd arrived home safely, I went into each of my sons' rooms and kissed them gently on their cheeks. How could I risk my safety when I had these two beautiful boys depending on me? I crawled back into bed. I cried into my pillow to keep from waking my husband.

Sadly, that was not the last time my obsession with weight would put my safety at risk. Just a few weeks later, thirty minutes into a strength workout at the gym, I felt a pain rip through my chest. Immediately, I dropped the weights and sat down. My heart was beating hard and my fingers went numb. Having never experienced anything like that before, I could only assume that it was related to the two fat-burning capsules I'd ingested an hour earlier. The warnings on the bottle cautioned that adverse reactions were possible, but I'd chosen to ignore them. I couldn't ignore them any longer.

The debate in my head began, "Do I push through the pain and try to salvage the rest of my workout, or do I go to the hospital?" I decided to go to the hospital.

Once there, I found myself sitting across from an intake nurse asking me what the problem was. An accurate answer would have been, "I'm suffering from a severe case of insecurity and bad judgement resulting in the ingestion of a fat burning herbal concoction sold to me by a guy named Tyson whose arms were as thick as my waist." Instead, I said, "My chest hurts."

When it was time to see the doctor, I told him about the diet pills. I expected him to give me a lecture. Instead, he rolled his eyes and said: "That was a dumb thing to do, don't do it again." Before he sent me home, he administered an EKG as a precaution and told me to make better choices.

I got home to find Nate dressing for work.

"How could you be so stupid?" he asked after I told him where I'd just spent the last two hours. "Honestly Marci, that was a completely idiotic thing to do." I felt like a child being scolded. He asked me for the pills. I told him I had thrown them away and promised never to take them again.

I lied.

A week later, I swallowed the two pills that I had stashed in a shoe at the back of my closet. I had kept them for an emergency. In this instance, the emergency was catching a glimpse of my once perfectly toned stomach in my bathroom mirror. Seeing the extra bit of softness around my tummy had thrown me into a panic. Twenty minutes after taking the pills, the chest pain was back! This time I told Nate about it right away. He called me a liar and ordered me to give him the rest of the pills. This time they really were gone, but he didn't believe me. He started rummaging through my drawers, in my closet, and under the bed. When he was mostly convinced that they were gone, he gave me a stern warning to never try anything that stupid again. He spent the next hour calming me down and reassuring me that I was not having a heart attack. Once again, I begged for his forgiveness. This time I got it without the sexual caveat.

I never touched another fat burner, but I was still undereating and over-exercising. I was also experiencing chronic pain in my upper abdominal area. Stomach pain wasn't new for me. My surgeries back west had left me with moderate chronic pain and a prescription for the narcotic Oxycontin. Over two years, my doctor had steadily increased the dose until I was taking what he referred to as an "SL" dose of medication. It was his polite way of saying a "Shitload."

When I expressed my disdain for the Oxycontin, which made me sleepy, the doctor switched me to Methadone. He believed it to be the best medication for chronic pain. It helped for a while but my pain started to get worse. I was sent to a gastroenterologist who discovered something worrisome on my liver. Fearing it could be cancerous, he scheduled me for surgery. I was 34-years-old and had already cheated death once. I couldn't help but wonder if I'd get another chance or, more importantly, if I deserved one.

My biggest fear was leaving my boys without a mother. At three and six, would they remember me if I didn't survive the surgery? Who'd set up obstacle courses for them in the park and scavenger hunts around the house? Who'd make them playdough out of flour and finger-paint out of pudding? Who'd keep the music on for them to dance to?

In my mania, I'd felt that I was doing the best I could for my boys while burning the candle at both ends. I was now slowly realizing that a better mom would be taking care of herself. If I truly wanted to do my best for them, wouldn't I be feeding my body the foods it needed and giving it all of the proper sleep that it required? I worried that what I'd put my body through was setting me up for disaster with my liver surgery and that some-how it would deny my boys the lifetime of unconditional love, the safety and support, that they so deserved.

A few days before my operation, I wrote each of my sons a letter, tell-ing them how deeply I loved them and how proud I was to be their mom. I encouraged them to follow their dreams and promised to always watch over them. It was heart-wrenching to write. I left the letters with Nate in the event that I did not survive the surgery. Fortunately, they were not necessary.

I spent ten days in hospital recovering from a successful liver resection. The doctors assured me that their concerns were unfounded and I was healthy. They explained that it would take my liver several weeks to regener-ate. I was alive and in good health.

But I wasn't okay. I had spent years pushing myself to extremes, physi-cally and psychologically. Being forced to moderate my life threw me for a loop. I wasn't prepared for the emotional toll it would take. Years of sleep deprivation and under-eating now caught up with me. The reality of every-thing I had experienced to that point hit me all at once. All of my losses, my health scares, my fuck-ups, and the changes in my marriage, all the pain and grieving I'd been avoiding for all that time, now overwhelmed me.

My recovery period should have lasted eight weeks. It took a year. I used to spend hours of my day working out at the gym. Suddenly I found it impossible to lift myself off the couch. Another mom in my neighborhood was taking the boys to and from school. I didn't have the energy. I was also out-of-control binging on food. The eating disorder that used to deny me food was now forcing it on me.

My compulsion to overeat started two days after my liver surgery. Late that night, I crawled out of my hospital bed and snuck into the hallway looking for cookies I had seen on a lunch cart earlier in the day. The large scar on my abdomen, shaped like a hockey stick, was incredibly sore, but my need to eat was overpowering and impossible to ignore.

Once I was home and sticking to my couch, I started putting on weight. My body was in survival mode after being starved for so long. I was hang-ing onto every calorie and fat gram I consumed. The weight gain was embarrassing for me even though no one else noticed it. But I couldn't stop eating. Food was filling the compulsive void that my newfound lack of sex had left behind. It was also a weapon I used against myself. If my body made me attractive to men and I wanted to stop that from happening, I'd stuff myself and become invisible.

I tried my best to be present for my kids but as the days passed, I found it increasingly difficult to focus on anything other than what I had eaten, what I was eating, or what I was going to eat. It wasn't unusual for me eat a huge bowl of ice cream and a bag of cookies before 9 a.m. After getting rid of the empty containers, I'd promise myself that I wouldn't eat for the rest of the day. Within the hour, I'd be back in the kitchen wolfing down a loaf of bread with all of the sandwich meat I'd bought for the boys' lunches. Even garbage wasn't off limits. I'd rummage through the trash to retrieve a half-eaten brownie I'd thrown away earlier. I ate foods straight from the freezer without giving them time to defrost. I'd burn my mouth on foods I was too impatient to let cool.

Nate had watched me struggle with my eating disorder for years, but even he was shocked at how much and how often I was eating.

"How is it humanly impossible for you to have consumed as much as you did in such a short period of time?" he asked after finding several chocolate bar wrappers in the trash.

My over-eating got so extreme that he reinstalled our child safety gates to prevent my middle-of-the-night binges. He thought that the sound of the gate would wake him and he could stop me from going to the kitchen. But he was a heavy sleeper, and I was quiet.

I'm not sure how long I was in this state. It might have been a year. It could have been two. I felt weighed down by failure and exhausted by emotional and physical pain. I remember lying on the couch, my stomach sore from the leftover pizza I had consumed, thinking, "I can't do this anymore."

I didn't want to die, but I didn't feel like I had the strength to live. I had given up on myself and the hope of ever feeling okay again.

All that kept me going was my boys. They deserved a mother who was healthy and happy and could give them the love I'd always tried to give. So, I tried again to get help.

One day, while they were at school, I walked into the crisis clinic at the hospital and begged someone to help me. I poured my soul out to the eating disorder specialist on call. I told him how depressed I was feeling, how disappointed I was with myself, and how I could not stop eating despite how physically ill it made me.

He looked at me smugly and said, "I don't believe you. If you were really eating that much, you'd be fatter."

He actually thought I was lying. He thought someone had walked into the hospital with a mortifying tale about being desperate and disgusted with herself, and she was embellishing. Why would anyone do that?

He turned me away. I sobbed all the way home. I grabbed two bags of chips from the kitchen pantry and started researching eating disorder treatment centers. I found a new program offered through a hospital in my area. After a few deep breaths, I dialed the number.

CHAPTER EIGHTEEN

Breaking up with ED

Do you eat pebbles?
Do you eat chalk?
Do you eat sand?

"WERE THEY SERIOUS?" I asked myself, sitting in the waiting room of the eating disorder treatment program. I had been given a questionnaire to fill out as part of my assessment, and these particular questions caught me off guard.

I answered, "No," and figured maybe I wasn't as crazy as I had thought. While I knew I needed help, there was a part of me hoping they'd tell me that my situation wasn't dire and then offer me a quick fix to get me back on track.

Unfortunately, that wasn't the case. After reviewing my answers and chatting with me for twenty minutes, the clinical psychologist shared her recommendation,

"I recommend that you join our intensive treatment program. You'll be starting tomorrow."

I was stunned. The treatment center offered two different styles of treatment. The out-patient program was a group format that took place five hours a day, three days a week, and ran for three months. The intensive program also ran for three months but required patients to be there for twelve hours a day, five days a week. I was supposed to go into the intensive program. I already hated the fact that I wouldn't be home for my kids after school on certain days. I refused to extend that to the entire week.

Despite their best efforts to convince me otherwise, I chose the less intensive option. I was instructed to show up at 1 p.m. the following day. It felt sudden but, in reality, it had been a long time coming. I had actually been on the program's waiting list for nearly a year. It wasn't an easy wait; while I hunkered down in the hopes that a spot would open up, I binged and binged. I found that while asking for help for an eating disorder was hard, getting help was a million times harder. It's hard to ask someone with this sort of serious disorder to wait so long for support. I also knew that if I didn't take advantage of this opportunity, it could be a long time before anything opened up again: I had reached out to several eating disorder programs before this one, and each had a waiting list that went on for years.

Walking into the room on my first day, I found eight women sitting in a semi-circle, and all of them were thinner and younger than me. There's nothing less comfortable for a woman struggling with body image than to be the oldest and fattest person in the room. The others were battling anorexia nervosa, whereas I was deep into the overeating part of my disorder. Despite my binges, I was still on the lower end of a healthy weight range. Even though I knew this, I still believed that I was overweight. Looking around the room, I wondered if it had been a mistake to enter the program. But I found a seat, took a deep breath, and waited for things to start.

Each day was comprised of four classes, with an hour break for dinner. In the first class, all of the participants took turns sharing how they were feeling. The class was led by a dietitian and a therapist. They would offer advice and suggestions while the rest of us were encouraged to chime in. I had mixed emotions about this. Did I really want advice about my eating disorder from someone who also had an eating disorder?

The whole concept of group therapy was new and, on occasion, stressful for me. Even though we were all in the same program, we were each at different stages of the recovery process. My favorite part of the group dynamic was the freedom and acceptance I felt when I first shared my stories about the most shameful parts of my disorder. I remember how sick with anxiety

I felt as I confessed to eating food out of the garbage. I expected to be met with looks of disgust or judgment. Instead, the other women looked at me with expressions that said, "Yup, me too." I didn't feel crazy or alone.

I also loved being around people who had several weeks of strong recovery under their belts. Listening to their stories was inspiring. Twenty-year old Raquel quickly became a beacon of hope for me. She was vibrant and energetic and seemed genuinely happy. It was hard for me to believe that just a few months earlier, she'd been feeling just as hopeless and desperate as I was. Raquel's recovery gave me the incentive I needed to give the program a fair shot.

I did find one thing particularly frustrating about the group setting. While hearing stories of recovery was inspiring, it was incredibly stressful to hear about the struggles. I was aware that the whole point of the group was for us to offer support to one another, but I felt triggered by a few of the participants. A twenty-something woman named Sarah was the most challenging for me. When I joined, she had been in the group for a week, but it wasn't her first time there. A year earlier, she had quit the program, deciding that she wasn't ready. They had let her come back but it was clear she was still not approaching it constructively. Instead of trying to focus on a healthier eating plan, she'd share the sneaky things she'd been doing to avoid it.

"I like to chew my food and then spit it out!" she told us one day, "That way I get to enjoy the flavor without the calories!"

When I heard that, I was disgusted. Then I started thinking it was actually quite clever, and I regretted not having tried it before starting treatment. I even considered trying it when I got home that night. Fortunately, that thought was short-lived. I remembered why I was there in the first place. My kids needed a healthy, happy mom, and I was determined to be that for them.

A week later, Sarah left the program again. This time, it wasn't by choice. Upon acceptance, each patient is given a two-week period to get onboard with the rules and regulations. If they can't toe the line after two weeks, they time on asked to leave. With a long list of people desperate to get in, it didn't make sense to waste on people who weren't willing or ready to comply.

The diets were very similar for all of us. We were given identical lists of foods we could choose from on a daily basis. The only thing that varied between patients was quantity and calorie count. Each of us, depending on our weight goals, were given personalized diet plans that told us exactly how much of each food to eat. Unlike the other members of my group, I didn't have any weight to gain. I also didn't have any to lose. My goal was to maintain the weight I was at.

I was the only person in the group who was allowed to exercise, but in moderation. That meant no more trips to the gym in the middle of the night. I was permitted to work out between the hours of 9 a.m. and 7 p.m., for a reasonable amount of time and only four days a week.

Moderation was a foreign concept to me. I was either starving myself while going to the gym every night at 2 a.m., or binging on cookies while avoiding the gym completely. Finding a middle ground was difficult.

The diet was also a challenge. It was complete shocking. It blew apart every diet rule I had ever been given. Everything I had been taught over the years about "good foods" and "bad foods" was out the window. It was incredibly confusing and really difficult to wrap my brain around.

We were not permitted to eat any foods that were labelled low fat, fat free, lite, or sugar free. Up to that point I had only been buying foods that were fat free and sweetened with Aspartame. Eating things like full fat yogurt and jam with real sugar was scary. But things went from scary to horrifying when I was handed the list of "foods to include."

On this piece of paper were three columns, labelled A, B, and C. I was instructed to eat one item from each column every day. It was made clear to me that I could not choose the same items every day and would need to make my way down the list until I had eaten all of them. All other proteins, fruits, and vegetables were listed on a separate sheet of paper. Substitutions could be made for health or religious concerns, but only at the discretion of the dietitian.

One glance at the foods listed made me feel sick to my stomach. There wasn't one item in any of the columns that I felt safe eating. If I had been asked to make a list of all of the foods I'd never eat again in my life, it would look almost identical. The thought kept running through my mind: "I'm going to get so fat!"

A.

Yogurt   Apple sauce
Cottage cheese   Mayonnaise
Peanut butter   Butter
Maple syrup   Avocado

B.

2 pieces of fried chicken/ fish   Popsicle
3 slices of cheese   Bagel
¾ cup of granola   2 pieces of toast
Salad dressing   Small bag of pretzels
4 chicken fingers   Small bag of potato chips
2 slices of pizza   5 pieces of licorice
Chocolate pudding cup

C

3 cookies   Ice cream cone
10 gummy bears   Chocolate bar
Slice of pie   Brownie
Slice of cake   Rice crispy square
Ice cream sundae

I started crying, right there in front of the other women and the leaders of the group. I was crying over pretzels and pancakes. I knew it was ridiculous, but it also validated my need for the treatment program.

I knew I had to comply but didn't know if I'd be able to. Nate was equally confused with my new eating plan.

"Can't you get the same number of calories from eating more protein and less junk food?" he asked when I got home.

I thought it was a valid question. I knew I would be much more comfortable eating an extra piece of chicken than I would a Snickers bar. I called the hospital and spoke to the dietician about it. She made her position very clear. "These are the rules," she explained. "If you follow them, you can stay, if you don't, someone else will be happy to take your spot." I could feel myself starting to cry again. I really wanted to get healthy, but I was so afraid of gaining weight.

I eventually came to grips with the fact that if I was to have a chance in hell of being happy again, I needed to try things their way.

The next day started off promising. I managed to add a few new items to my diet, like full fat yogurt, buttered toast, and cheese. I was feeling hopeful until it was time for dessert. I chose to eat three Oreo cookies. Never in my life had I ever been able to eat just three cookies. Usually I'd avoided them altogether until I couldn't resist anymore . . . and then I would allow myself to eat just two more, promising myself they'd be the last cookies I'd ever eat. As soon as the last bite would be swallowed, I'd feel disgusted with my lack of willpower and punish myself by eating a dozen more.

I wondered if this time I'd be able to stop at just three. The answer was no.

I ate the three Oreos and then continued eating more from the bag until I'd finished off an even ten. What the fuck was wrong with me?! I felt completely discouraged. At that point it seemed pointless to even try to stay on track. Before I knew it, I was experiencing a full-on binge. I ate until I felt too sick to eat anymore.

I barely slept that night, worried that I was going to get kicked out of the program. I prepared myself for the worst when I walked into the dietitian's office and confessed my food sins. I was pleasantly surprised when she explained that binging was an expected part of the process. It was the reason we were given the grace period. They recognized that changing our entire mindset around food wasn't going to happen overnight. I was relieved but also concerned that my mindset would never change.

Luckily, I was wrong. A week later, as I was leaving my basement after a forty-five-minute workout on my elliptical machine, I felt something in me click. I literally felt a change come over me, bringing me feelings of peace and strength.

Maybe it had to do with the fact that my sleeping and eating patterns had become much less erratic. Maybe it was the support I was getting from people in the program. Whatever it was, it was powerful and life-changing. Suddenly, instead of being afraid of the foods on my list, I was excited about them. I was amazed at how good food tasted when I allowed myself to eat what I was craving instead of settling for "safer" substitutes. Before the program, when I craved chocolate, I'd find a fat free, sugarless substitute that shared chocolate's color and texture, but none of its flavor. I was always unsatisfied, which is why I'd continue to eat. Now, by actually eating the foods I wanted, I didn't need to overeat them.

My kids were happy too. It was fun for them to watch me eat and enjoy things like ice cream and French fries. I think they mostly just loved having a more relaxed version of their mom. I'm sure it was easier for my husband, too. Being married to someone battling an eating disorder is incredibly challenging. As much as he wanted to understand what I was going through, he never could. I have no doubt that at times he felt helpless. I know he felt frustrated. I don't blame him. I was in recovery for all of us.

The treatment program helped me understand the root of my disorder and gave me a sense of clarity I had never experienced before. For the first time since I started this relationship with my eating disorder, I was ready to end it.

My favorite class in the program was Art Therapy. One of the exercises I had to do was write a letter to my eating disorder. I expected my letter to be angry, but I surprised myself when it ended up being a Thank You letter instead:

Dear ED,

Thank you. Thank you for showing up when my brother was dying. When the pain was so deep and so strong, I thought I might die too. Thank you for giving me something else to focus on besides his empty room and my empty heart. Thank you for staying with me for years afterwards when life seemed so cruel and unfair and facing it was just too hard . . . you gave me somewhere to hide.

Thank you for tricking me into thinking you were gone so I could get married and for hiding when I was pregnant, so I could enjoy my children, and so my mom could die with a sense of peace, knowing that I would be okay.

And thanks for coming back when life got tough again, when the traumas hit fast and hard and I needed to escape . . . thanks for taking the blame when I lost myself and did things I will forever regret.

Thank you.

But now you need to go.

I know it's hard to take me seriously since I've tried to break up with you before, only to reach out to you each and every time when things got tough. I don't blame you for wanting to stay. Life was never boring when we were together. It's just that I feel hurt that you saw how much pain you were causing me and you still refused to leave. If you loved me, you'd have let me go years ago.

It's taken me 20 years to see that with all that you've given me, you've taken so much more. I can't begin to imagine how many people you've pushed out of my life and how many experiences I've missed out on just because you wanted me all to yourself. You systematically knocked down my dreams like bowling pins, leaving me feeling scared and alone. No matter how many people told me they loved me, yours was the only voice I heard, telling me I wasn't thin enough, pretty enough, smart enough, that I wasn't a good enough person to merit a place in the world, especially after my mom and Billy died. I didn't deserve to be here taking up a spot that should have belonged to one of them.

I thought we were done in Vancouver when I was so sick and it didn't seem like I would pull through, when the doctors thought I'd never get to hold my son again or watch him grow up, and the son in my belly had been taken away without ever meeting his mommy. I swore I'd never waste another second of my time on you . . . but at the first sign of weakness, you were back.

Well, I'm not weak now. I am strong and getting stronger by the minute. I don't need you. I'm ready to face my life and begin healing. I have the tools I need to block you out forever. I thought you took my pain away but you were just burrowing down deep inside of me, where you could cause the most damage. I'm ready to live my life without you. I hope that you will let me go without too much of a fight. You served your purpose and now it's time to let me fly on my own.

This time, it really is goodbye.

That program changed my life, or at least it gave me the support and the tools I needed to help me change it myself. By the time the three months were over, I was sleeping properly, eating properly, and feeling comfortable in my skin. Surprisingly, I hadn't gained a single pound. I learned that I could eat all kinds of foods, even ones that had no redeeming qualities aside from tasting delicious, and my weight would not be impacted. It wasn't cake that was causing the huge fluctuations in my body, but the constant cycle of fasting and binging. I left the program with a freedom from the fear of food that had been weighing me down for years. It was exhilarating.

Once I was finally feeling optimistic about my future, I was ready to take the next step. It was time to get off pain medication.

In total, I had spent six years on heavy-duty narcotics. I hated feeling dependent on them. I was also still feeling pain, which led me to believe they weren't helping me all that much anyway. I met with a gastroenterologist who suggested that it was the narcotics that were causing my pain instead of treating it. Drugs like Oxycontin and Methadone are most effective when used briefly rather than over an extended period of time. He explained that those drugs wreaked havoc on the stomach and he strongly believed that I would feel better once I was free of them.

Really? As soon as I heard that there was even a possibility that my pain could be relieved if I got off the meds, I was ready to go for it. I spoke with my pain management doctor, but he was not as convinced. In his opinion, Methadone was such a difficult drug to wean from, it made more sense to just keep taking it.

Hell no. Why would I want to stay dependent on a drug that could actually be causing my pain? I made it clear that I wanted to start the process of weaning. For reasons he never explained, he didn't support my decision and left me to do it on my own. After that conversation, I never spoke with him again.

I set a goal to be off my medication by my mother's birthday, six weeks away. I had read enough about the process to know that the period of withdrawal that I was about to experience was going to be a living hell. The thing is, I had been through hell before, and this was important enough to make one more trip.

For six weeks, I felt as if I had the worst flu of my life. My muscles ached, and I had pain running up and down my body. I was nauseous and exhausted yet unable to sleep. My skin crawled and my heart raced. Two of these weeks took place during March break, when both kids were home from school. I managed to keep how I was feeling a secret from them. After beating my eating disorder, I felt empowered to do anything.

The day of my mom's birthday came and, as planned, I was 100% medication free. When I told my gastroenterologist that I had taken his advice and kicked the drugs, he walked around his desk and gave me a giant hug. Then he scribbled something onto his prescription pad and told me to give it to my husband. It was a prescription for a fancy dinner. I was one of only three patients he'd ever had that successfully weaned off of Methadone. He was proud of me and wanted me to celebrate.

For the first time in as far back as I could remember, I was proud of myself. The fearless girl with the feisty spirit was fighting her way back. I was also finding my voice again, and it wasn't long before I was using it to make waves and ruffle feathers.

CHAPTER NINETEEN

Fit vs Fiction

"WE HAD AN ASSEMBLY at school today and you are *not* going to be very happy about it!" my youngest, who was in third grade, told me after school one day.

On leaving the treatment program a few years earlier, I'd hoped to never to think about food or body image issues ever again. I quickly discovered that unless I was completely removed from civilization, that wasn't going to happen. It became clear to me that from birth we are force-fed a steady diet of unrealistic beauty expectations that damage our self-worth and self-esteem. Most of us spend our entire lives as victims to diet fads and weight-loss scams in efforts to look the way we think we're supposed to look. Marketers spend billions of dollars convincing us that skinny is synonymous with pretty and that physical appearance is more important than physical fitness.

I was still exercising when I left the program, but my love affair with the fitness industry had ended. My recovery had shown me how shallow it was. Most fitness trainers measured success in losses of pounds and body-fat percentage instead of gains in strength and endurance. As a result, people were putting their health at risk in an effort to merely *look* healthy. I knew firsthand how deceiving physical appearance could be.

When I was training with Buff Bobby, I was constantly asked to share my diet and exercise routines with people who admired my dedication to fitness. I would tell them that I ate well and trained hard, which was total bullshit. If I had been honest, I would have said, "My trainer has me drinking a mere quarter cup of liquid a day, and I haven't eaten solid food in eight weeks." Instead, I chose to perpetuate the myth that the skinniest bodies were the healthiest and the most muscular bodies were the strongest.

Recovery had opened my eyes to the damage caused by these beauty and fitness myths, and I felt compelled to speak against them. My kids had seen my struggle, witnessed my recovery, and were now part of my rebellion.

"What happened at the assembly?" I asked.

My son told me that the school was introducing something called "The Healthy Schools Initiative." The goal was to encourage healthier eating among students. I had no problem with that, until he told me how they were going to do it.

The plan was to elect two students in each class, from kindergarten through seventh grade, as food monitors. Their job would be to examine their classmates' lunches to make sure they contained only healthy foods. The students who had healthy lunches were given raffle tickets for a prize draw at the end of each week. The children who didn't pass the inspection were not allowed to participate in the draw.

My son was right. I wasn't happy. I was furious. My anger only intensified as I learned more about this new program. During the assembly, a teacher yelled out a type of food and the students yelled back whether they were raffle-worthy or not.

"Is an apple okay?" she asked the crowd.

"Yes!" the kids shouted back.

"How about a cookie?" she asked next.

"No!" they shouted back.

I nearly lost my mind. How could anybody in the school system actually think that this was a good idea? The junior food police were not equipped with the knowledge to understand the nutritional value of foods. Even if they were, criticizing someone else's lunch is a horrible and dangerous idea.

I called the school and made it clear that my kids would not be participating in this ridiculous program. I planned on leaving it at that until other parents reached out to me for help.

The other parents knew of my body image advocacy because the former principal had allowed me to share my insights at the school a couple of years earlier. At that time, I'd been upset that schools were promoting weight loss as a major part of their health programs. Diet culture was impacting kids barely out of pre-school, and I wasn't going to just sit back and watch it happen.

The principal had invited me to speak to eighth graders. I was thrilled at the opportunity but didn't have anything prepared. I decided to keep it simple and spoke from the heart. By sharing my self-esteem struggles openly and honestly, I created an atmosphere that encouraged conversation, which is what I wanted. It didn't take long for the students to open up about the stresses they were feeling around the pressure to diet. It became clear that this was something kids *needed* to talk about. I walked away inspired and determined to keep speaking out.

This is why these parents contacted me about the impact of the new food initiative on their kids. Their concerns were justified. In an effort to avoid food shaming from their peers, their kids were stuffing their snacks into their pockets before going to the washroom and eating them privately. They wanted their treats but didn't want to be bullied. They also wanted their raffle tickets. While I understood that the school had the best of intentions, I also knew how dangerous it was to create shame around food.

I requested a meeting with the food initiative staff. I showed up armed with information supporting my position, supplied to me by an eating disorder specialist at the Toronto Children's Hospital. The meeting resulted in the program being axed. A few days later, I was summoned to the principal's office. I was informed that my actions had offended some of the teachers and that it would be better if I didn't talk about it or write about it in my blog.

I did both. Needless to say, I was never invited to speak at the school again.

I was disappointed by their reaction, but by that point I was already speaking at several other schools in my community and was confident about the positive impact that I was having. I also began contacting radio and television programs that I felt were promoting unhealthy beauty ideals for children. Some of these programs even asked me to make an appearance so that I could speak about eating disorders and kids' body image issues. Social media hadn't exploded yet, so it seemed like I was the only person speaking openly on the topic. I started receiving more media invitations.

My first television appearance on "The Mom Show," where I mentioned the Fit vs. Fiction body image workshops that I had designed. Fit vs. Fiction was a series of interactive seminars for students in grades one through twelve. The goal was to empower kids with the information and tools they needed to ignore the negative messages they were being inundated with by society, the media, and marketers. I loved working with these kids, and the workshops were a lot of fun for them: they included a ton of pictures, real life stories, and games. The students were encouraged to share their thoughts and feelings with the group or, afterwards, privately with me.

Somebody once asked me if I was worried by the idea that I wasn't reducing body image concerns for the kids – because they were so young, maybe I was actually introducing these issues. My answer? "Absolutely not." There were kids as young as five already in treatment for eating disorders. I will never forget the call I received from the mother of a kindergarten student who refused to wear her winter coat because she feared it made her look fat. My heart ached when the vice principal of a private school told me she had walked in on a group of eighth grade girls vomiting up their lunches in the school bathroom. I knew that when it came to encouraging positive relationships with our bodies, there was no such thing as too young.

Along with my workshops, I started a blog where I could speak my mind. One of my posts got picked up by *The Huffington Post*, and I was asked to join their team of bloggers which gave me access to a much larger audience. It also resulted in an invitation to New York City as a guest on the Fox show *Geraldo at Large*, hosted by the one and only Geraldo Rivera. Geraldo has a reputation for being unscrupulous and I saw nothing to prove any different.

My appearance on the show resulted from an article I had written called "Why I'm Not a Fit Mom Anymore." It was in response to a woman known on social media as "Fit Mom." She was a fitness professional passing herself off as a "regular mom" with three kids under ten years old. She claimed that she was able to attain the physique of a fitness model by finding simple ways to sneak little bits of exercise into her day. She posted a picture of herself and her kids and captioned it, "What's your excuse?" Some people found it inspiring. More people found it insulting. There was an insinuation that any mom who didn't have a body like hers wasn't trying hard enough.

I didn't believe her for a second. I knew what it took to look that way and hated that her message was making so many mothers feel insecure. In my rebuttal, I talked about the restrictive dieting and overtraining it took to look that toned and lean. I also explained why I would never again trade sleep and time with my children for rock hard abs and toned biceps. Geraldo's producer asked me to share my views on the show.

Unfortunately, as soon as I took my seat next to Geraldo, I learned his real motivation for having me there.

"Fit Mom is going to be joining us via satellite!" the producer informed me for the first time. He had purposely waited to share this information with me so I would be caught off guard.

"Feel free to cut her off whenever you want," Geraldo whispered to me with an off-putting smile.

They weren't interested in my opinion. They wanted a cat fight.

I had no interest in turning a message I strongly believed in into voyeuristic entertainment for Geraldo and his fans. I did my best to get through the frustrating interview while avoiding the heated conflict they were trying to create. Those efforts proved pointless when the show's editing team manipulated the footage in a way that brought their trumped-up narrative to life and made me look surprisingly aggressive. I suppose I should have known better.

I was disappointed, but no less determined. After reading about one too many female celebrities being criticized for not having perfect bodies and overhearing a group of pre-teen girls complaining about their own insecurities, I put my frustration into writing and published my body image rant.

Two radio stations contacted me as soon as it was published, requesting interviews. Both programs described me as an "angry activist." They weren't entirely wrong. I was angry. I was angry that hating our bodies had become second nature. But I was also hopeful that the tide was changing, little by little with more people speaking out. Here's my rant:

"We live in an image-obsessed, fat-phobic, one-size-fits-all, thin-is-in, skinny-jean wearing, thigh-gap measuring, binging and purging, body-fat freezing, rather-be-dead-than-eat-bread society where women are starving to be smaller and men are injecting themselves with poison to be bigger, and kids in pre-school are begging their parents not to send them to school because they think they're too fat to fit in.

And that pisses me off!

I'm offended by the magazines that use Photoshop and other tools of destruction to completely erase every wrinkle, line, or crease on their models' faces in an effort to create an unrealistic image of beauty that we'll spend our entire lives trying to attain but never will.

I'm angry at casting directors who cast 30-year-old women to play the wives of 60-year-old men because nobody would believe that a woman his own age could ever be attractive.

I feel sad for actresses with faces full of Botox and empty bellies, who spend more time with their trainers than their toddlers, and who when asked, "How do you stay so young looking?" respond with the lie, "I drink lots of water and do yoga twice a week."

I'm irritated by the entertainment industry that tells them it's what they have to do in order to stay relevant and employable.

I'm disgusted by the media outlets who criticize pregnant celebrities for getting "fat" while they're growing human beings in their bodies.

I'm worried about moms who allow years of negative messages telling them they're not good enough to affect the way they treat themselves and then inadvertently pass those same messages to their kids.

I'm heartsick for parents visiting their children in eating disorder clinics because, despite how many times they were told they needed to eat to be healthy, all they heard was society telling them they needed to starve themselves to be beautiful.

I'm frustrated with men's fitness magazines that perpetuate the myth that a real man is judged on the strength of his muscles instead of his character.

But I'm excited that people have started speaking out about the damage being done to our children by a society that idolizes the prettiest faces but ignores the most brilliant minds.

I feel hopeful when I speak at schools and hear the anger in the voices of the students as they learn how they're being manipulated by marketers, and I love when they realize that they have the power to reject this nonsense and the right to ask for something better.

I'm optimistic that the day is coming when our daughters would rather be elected president than crowned America's Next Top Model, and our sons understand that muscles don't mean manliness and being sensitive isn't for 'sissies.'

Self-worth shouldn't be measured in pounds."

After my radio interviews, I decided to call my treatment program and thank the people there for changing my life. The nurse who answered told me that she was literally reading my rant when I called! She was pleasantly surprised to find out I was a former patient and invited me to share my story with the present program participants. I was thrilled to do it. Eating disorders are widely misunderstood. Very few people understand the soul-crushing toll they take on the people battling them. I was honored and humbled to be able to shine a little light of hope.

My passion for the body image movement was limitless, but unfortunately, my funding was not. I was so focused on helping as many kids as I could, that I never turned down a request for help. That meant spending hours speaking at schools with small budgets and even accepting speaking engagements for free. I would work with parents and kids one-on-one and not charge them a dime. I found it impossible to ask parents for money when their children were struggling. I was a great speaker but a lousy businesswoman, and I knew it.

My situation was getting to be challenging. It turns out that you can turn your life around in important ways, as I did with my sexcapades and my eating disorder, and still find yourself in much the same place.

I was a full-time mom driving my sons to and from school every day and helping with their homework. I was also trying to keep Fit vs. Fiction going and looking for ways to make it more profitable. I thought I could do it all, but the self-doubt was creeping back in. Was it because I felt like I wasn't contributing enough to our family finances? Was it because I didn't feel like I was the homemaker I should have been? Or was it because I knew the truth about myself?

I was a fraud.

CHAPTER TWENTY

The Unwinding

"WHY IS THAT MAN looking at you?" my son asked me uncomfortably.

I had spent that afternoon presenting Fit vs. Fiction workshops to a group of high schoolers before picking my kids up from school. We stopped at the grocery store on our way home. As we turned down the cereal aisle, a man walked past us, turning his head to look back our way. He slowed his pace and kept his eyes on me until he reached the end of the aisle. Before turning the corner, he flashed me a quick smile.

"I have no idea," I told him. "Maybe he thinks I'm someone he knows."

I wasn't being completely honest. I did have an idea. Actually, I had a few ideas, and all of them filled me with anxiety.

When Nate got home from work, I told him what happened. This wasn't the first time I had told him about an uncomfortable glare or creepy smile I had gotten from a stranger while out with the kids. He remained unfazed, as always.

Even though it had been almost ten years since my husband and I had ended all of our sexual shenanigans, I was still haunted by them. I was terrified of the truth coming out. Whenever I did anything for Fit vs. Fiction that put me in the public eye, I half expected one of the scorned wives I had wronged to resurface and call me out over social media. I was still carrying so much shame. And the thought of my sons being hurt by my indiscretions was unbearable.

It was this last thought that raised my anxiety in the grocery store. The way that man looked at me had me wondering the same thing as my son: who was he? It's possible that he did have me confused with someone else, or that he was making a poor attempt at flirting, but my fear sent my thoughts in other directions.

"Did I have sex with him?" I tried to remember, "Did he pay me to dance for him?"

I stood in the middle of the grocery store, fully clothed, feeling completely naked and vulnerable. I was afraid he'd approach me and say something that would blow my cover and expose me as the harlot I used to be. I was relieved when we got through the checkout line without incident

My husband's response to my fears was always the same.

"Deny, deny, deny," he'd say. "Never admit to anything."

While that approach had always worked for him, it could never work for me. I had to pray it would never come up.

In the years following what I referred to as our "crazy time," Nate and I had become pretty good at playing the happily married couple. Both of our kids were high-level athletes. Their training and competition schedules kept us busy. My husband was a very involved dad. He took great pride in our sons' accomplishments and was at every game and tournament cheering them on. Supporting our children came naturally for both of us. Supporting each other was a different story.

Regular, daily responsibilities made it easy for us to avoid any major conflicts or confrontations. We co-existed in a way that seemed to work for a while. While there wasn't a lot of fighting, there also wasn't a lot of love. I was still dealing with unresolved resentment over the way I felt I had been manipulated when I was at my most vulnerable. I wanted to get past it, but whenever I'd want to talk about it, he'd brush it off and say, "I was young and stupid. Plus, it was years ago, get over it already!"

I wished I could. I truly wanted to get over it, but I couldn't. There was a huge part of me that still felt unwanted and unloved. Not talking about it wasn't going to make these feelings magically disappear. I needed to know that he regretted what had happened, and that it hurt him to know that I was hurting. But that wasn't the case.

I was aware that I had not been the perfect partner, but I seemed to be the only one in the relationship who felt bad about things. I wished I hadn't brought my eating disorder into our marriage. I wished I hadn't gotten sick out west and lost our baby, and I wished I had been strong enough to handle these losses better than I had. I regretted my part in everything that came after: the whole Cassidy show.

It was true that we couldn't go back in time, and I was willing to move forward if I could feel safe with him again. But he was busy. Nate explained that while he agreed that our marriage was in trouble, he had priorities, and I was barely making the list.

"Maybe when the kids are older and don't need us as much, that'll change," he said.

We continued on this path for another couple of years. During that time, my self-confidence started to slip. A weird dynamic had evolved between my husband, the boys, and me. I was starting to feel like the odd man out. Nate and I did our best to keep the problems in our marriage from affecting our kids but his lack of emotion made any feeling that I expressed seem oversensitive and excessive. The three of them would roll their eyes and look at each other— "There she goes again!"

I felt lonelier and lonelier. I started turning down opportunities to share my body image workshops. I felt it would be hypocritical to preach about self-esteem while mine was plummeting. Nate had a subtle way of making me feel less competent than he was, and he didn't care if anyone was watching. After a while, I started questioning my own abilities and intelligence. Looking back, I feel horrible at how stressed I'd make my boys when I'd have to drive them somewhere on the highway. I had developed an almost paralyzing fear of getting lost and would start to panic when I thought I had taken a wrong turn. My husband would draw maps for me, saying that my sense of direction was so bad even a GPS system couldn't help me.

My self-esteem was so low I was afraid to put gas in my car. I had started driving later in life, and Nate was the only person who ever took the car to the gas station, so I'd never done it myself. Now that I wanted to, I couldn't. I was so afraid of making a mistake that I wouldn't try. My kids, who had seen me recover from my eating disorder and become a warrior in the body image field, were now watching me lose that strength and weaken again. I tried to hide it from them but I couldn't always manage.

Just before leaving on a family vacation to visit Nate's parents on the coast, I felt a sudden, intense pain on the left side of my face. It was unlike anything I had experienced in the past. I visited a nearby clinic and was diagnosed with Trigeminal Neuralgia.

Trigeminal Neuralgia is a chronic pain disorder that affects the trigeminal nerve, which carries sensation from the face to the brain. Its main symptom is excruciating pain. I'm not sure how I ended up developing it, but it made life miserable for a few months. After taking so long to recover from my liver surgery, I refused to let this keep me from parenting my children. I would drive my youngest to soccer practice and wait for him in the car, sobbing in pain. TN is a chronic disorder and I consider myself extremely lucky to have recovered from it. My marriage, however, was permanently affected.

After an unusually painful morning, I'd gone to see my doctor. I texted my husband after my appointment. He got home late from work that night without ever having responded. When I asked him why I hadn't heard back from him, he told me he just hadn't thought of me. Hearing that hurt more than anything.

"I got tired of your pain," he would later admit.

I understood. I was sure he was tired of it. I was tired of it. I was fucking exhausted. I didn't blame him for checking out. I just knew there was no coming back from it. I knew that our chances of ever again feeling connected to each other were gone.

That said, I wasn't ready to leave. My rationale was that since he wasn't physically abusive or cheating on me, I couldn't leave. It seemed selfish to break up my family just because I was miserable. People are often afraid of trading the evils they know for evils they don't know. They find safety in the familiar, even if the familiar is unhappy. That was me.

We continued on together in the exact same way for another two years. There wasn't a single hug, or kiss, or hand held in all that time. I was back to sleeping on the couch. It was my decision to move out of our bed. I found it too hard to be sitting up in bed crying to myself while he slept peacefully next me, unbothered by the state of our relationship. I made sure I hid my blanket and pillow out of sight before the kids came downstairs. I was still trying to be the perfect mom but felt like I was failing miserably. I'd break down in tears whenever I'd think that I had disappointed the boys in any way. Buying the wrong kind of juice or screwing up a meal felt catastrophic. I wanted to be strong again but I was losing the battle. Those old demons – the doubts that I had about deserving to take up space in the world – started calling out to me once more.

* * *

I had just dropped both of my sons off at their respective high schools. I made sure, as always, that we played music in the car and that I sang along with them. I also made sure to laugh at something, anything, at least once during the drive, so they wouldn't see the tears I was fighting to hold back.

"Don't cry. Don't fucking cry," I'd repeated in my head, over and over. "Don't. Fucking. Cry."

I knew I had to keep it together until I was alone in the car. Then, with both boys safely at school, I could let it out. It hurt. It physically hurt, letting all of that emotion out of my body. My heart was racing, my chest felt tight, and my shoulders ached from the tension they'd been holding in.

And then I saw it, the concrete overpass that I drove under every morning after dropping them off at school. I hated myself for thinking what I was thinking, but I was thinking it anyway. It was a way out. A way to stop the tears, to find peace, to get some rest. I felt like I'd spent my entire life fighting. I was always fighting for something or against something, always trying to get through something or over something. My soul was exhausted. What if I turn my steering wheel just a little more to the right as I got closer, and stepped on the gas a little bit harder? What if I closed my eyes and let the metal hit the concrete?

"Would it hurt?" I wondered. "Would it be quick, or would I suffer?"

It wasn't the first morning I'd had those thoughts, or even the fifteenth, but this time was different. Until then, I'd always felt that no matter how desperate I felt, I could never purposely leave my children. I knew what it was like to live motherless, and I couldn't do that to my own kids. But that day I couldn't help feeling they would be okay without me. Maybe even be better off.

But, like every morning, my steering wheel stayed straight and I made it to the other side, alive and unharmed. I'd love to say that it was a will to live, even just a weak one, that kept me from demolishing my car and ending my life, but it wasn't. I just didn't want to piss off the people who would be waiting for me on the other side. So many of the people I loved most were already gone, and if there was some kind of afterlife, they'd be furious with me for killing myself. The thought of disappointing them was unbearable to me. So, I kept driving.

My plan for the rest of today was to stop at the grocery store, buy a bunch of junk food that would satisfy my cravings for starch and salt and sugar in the short term but ultimately leave me feeling sick and ashamed of myself, crying some more, and then washing my face, fixing my hair, and putting on a little makeup before picking my sons up from school at 3:00 p.m.

I got to the grocery store, grabbed a cart, and reminded myself to breathe. My cart filled up with onion rolls and crackers. I grabbed three boxes of cookies and made sure I got something healthy: a few cans of tuna and sliced turkey to eat with the onion rolls. Next, it was the frozen food aisle for vegetables and ice cream. As I stood looking through the freezer doors, I could feel a combination of excitement and anxiety. I was excited at the idea of eating junk food, things I knew were bad for me. I was anxious because I would hate myself afterward and find some way to punish myself and repent.

I moved to the bulk section where I filled bags with chocolate mints, Whoppers, and licorice all-sorts. I made my way to the checkout counter and was greeted with a big "Hello!" from the cashier who had worked there as long as I could remember.

"I really need a break," she confided with a tired smile.

I smiled back, "You and me both."

"You? You're always full of light and positivity! I wish I had half your energy!"

"I'm pretty exhausted," I said quietly, feeling the tears start to well.

She stopped processing my order and asked if I was okay. I assured her that it had just been a tough morning.

"All I know is that when I see you, I see a woman who is vibrant, cheerful, and vivacious."

I left the store completely confused. I was not vibrant. I'd been crying all morning. I was not cheerful. I had to stop twenty-seven times in the thirty minutes I'd been here just to breathe deeply. How vivacious could I be when I was about to spend the next few hours sitting on my couch, stuffing my face, watching pre-recorded episodes of *Law & Order* and *Top Chef*?

My emotions overwhelmed me and I started sobbing again. I drove home feeling disoriented with a brutal headache coming on. As I put the groceries away, my head pounded and I started crying uncontrollably. I felt completely broken, used up, and drained of all strength. "Cheerful." "Vibrant." "Vivacious." Is that really how that woman saw me? How was that possible? It had been a million years since I'd felt that way.

I collapsed on the floor, an emotional wreck. I couldn't take feeling so sad. I couldn't handle feeling like such a failure. I didn't think I had strength left for another day. I felt I could stay in that position forever. Then I started to worry that my kids would notice my swollen eyes from crying and I knew I had to try to stop.

I dragged myself to the bathroom to wash my face. The cold water felt good. When I lifted my head from the sink, I saw something that changed everything.

CHAPTER TWENTY-ONE

Enough

A WIFE, A MOM, A STRIPPER, a slut, a motherless daughter, an abandoned sister, a bereaved parent, a victim, a jezebel, a fighter, a failure, and a survivor. I saw them all staring back at me in the bathroom mirror, all of the women I am and used to be.

For years, my reflection had been unfamiliar to me. I'd look at myself and wonder what I was seeing. I knew what I was supposed to see, but I had become so detached from that person that my reflection was unrecognizable.

In that moment, however, through blood shot eyes and tear-stained cheeks, I saw myself again. I saw all of the good, the bad, and the very ugly parts I'd loved and loathed for almost forty-five years. A strange feeling of peace came over me, washing away some of the critical voices in my head and replacing them with hints of compassion and forgiveness.

"Enough," said the voice in my head, and with that the tears stopped flowing and the pain in my head started to ease.

At that moment, I didn't know exactly what I was going to do, but I knew things were about to change. I put away the binge food, went into my basement, blared '80s music through my headphones and danced. Years before, dancing to Donna Summer and Gloria Gaynor on the shag rug in my family's living room had helped me escape the tension I felt brewing between my soon-to-be-divorced parents. It had been a long time since I had danced that way, and it felt amazing.

In the hours before I had to pick my kids up from school, I tried to figure out my next move. I found one of my old journals and started writing down questions:

What do I want?

What do I need?

What's holding me back from being happy?

What can I do today to set change in motion?

I didn't have the answers, but just asking the questions felt hopeful. Before I knew it, it was time to pick my kids up from school. I drove past that familiar underpass, smiled, and thought, "Not today."

I would love to say that as soon as I got home, I told my husband that I was done with the bullshit and wanted a divorce. The truth is that I don't remember exactly how or when I told him that I wanted to end our marriage. I do remember that he wasn't happy about it. He suggested we try couples therapy. It would be our second attempt at counselling after seeing someone very briefly and without success a few years earlier.

Despite believing that Nate's interest in saving our marriage had more to do with not wanting the hassles of divorce than with wanting to keep me, I agreed to set up an appointment. I knew that it was going to be a waste of time because, by that point, it was clear that our relationship couldn't – and more importantly, shouldn't – be salvaged. As it turned out, our therapist felt just the same as I did.

"I think Marci feels trapped," he mentioned during one of our sessions.

He was right. I did.

He also said that we had been through more than a lifetime's worth of major challenges in our twenty-four years together, and the damage was severe. For there to be any chance of repairing things, both of us would have to be willing to revisit these experiences, acknowledge them, and take ownership of the roles we each played in them. This went against my husband's "deny and get over it" method of dealing with difficult issues.

During our month or two of therapy, we took a trip to Montreal over the Christmas holidays to visit my sister. My relationship with my sister had been challenging for our entire lives. I think the seven-year age gap was a big part of that. Despite having shared many of the same childhood and family traumas, the age difference made it difficult for us to connect and relate to one another. Over the years, we tried to get along, but our efforts never seemed to last very long. A series of events led to us cutting all ties with each other for close to eight years. I missed her, but was resigned to the idea that our relationship wasn't meant to be. Then we unexpectedly ran into each other at a Pointer Sisters concert in Montreal on June 14, 2014. My mom had died on June 14, 1998. It seemed like fate. We reconnected.

This trip, two years later, was our first opportunity to spend real time together since our childhood. Lori arranged for us to spend a night at a hotel so we could stay up all night talking. I shared my marriage problems with her. She wasn't surprised. I had shared some of these things with her after my first child was born, but that time was such a blur that I had completely forgotten about what I'd confessed to her. It seems that I spilled my guts to her about all of Nate's extremely questionable behavior and what it had done to our marriage.

I asked my sister if she remembered how I felt at that time and why I didn't leave him then.

"You were devasted," she explained, "but Mommy had just died, you and I weren't on great terms, you had just given birth to a premature baby, and were living across the country from everyone you knew. Where were you going to go?"

It felt good to have my sister back. When I returned home, Nate and I saw our therapist a couple more times and decided to call it quits.

I remember the exact night we made that decision. We had gone to a pub to talk. I just looked at him and said, "I'm done. Are you done?"

He said, "Yeah, I think I'm done too."

Then we raised our glasses and toasted to making it through twenty-four years together.

I felt sad. I was absolutely sure that breaking up was the right decision: the damage to our marriage, whether through life's ups and downs or our own behavior, was impossible to repair. But sitting across from my husband at that moment, I couldn't help but think of our very first date and the courtship that followed. Despite some doubts and fears, we had been optimistic and hopeful that we'd beat the odds and live happily ever after. Twenty-four years later, while toasting the ending of our marriage, I couldn't help but think about the good parts, and there definitely were good parts. Even the worst marriage has its moments, and ours was far from the worst. The best part for us was getting to be parents to our boys. We will always feel incredibly lucky for that. As for the rest, we both wanted things to be different, but we also knew they never could be. I felt proud that we were letting each other go and that we'd be able to head off wherever life would take us.

We decided to tell the boys we were splitting up a little earlier than we had planned. We told them on May 2, 2016. I remember because it was the same date my mother had asked my father for a divorce thirty-six years earlier. It was also my father's birthday. My mother's gift to him that year was freedom from his responsibilities as a husband and a father.

Our sons were now teenagers and well established in their respective schools. Both boys were competing in sports and had big tournaments coming up. Nate and I were a bit delusional when it came to how we thought they'd react. We expected them to be upset by the news, but we really didn't think they'd be surprised. While we weren't the kind of couple that yelled and screamed at each other, we had not shown each other affection in years. I knew that our kids felt the tension between us. We sat them down in the living room and were as direct as possible.

Just thinking about that day makes my heart hurt. I had spent every minute since they were born trying to protect them from being hurt, and there I was being the cause of it. Seeing your children in pain is horrible and knowing you're the reason they're hurting is unbearable.

I suddenly realized that as dysfunctional as my marriage was, it was all they knew. I felt horribly guilty. I may have been miserable in my marriage, but did that give me the right to turn my kids' lives upside down? Would a better mother have waited until they were at least off to university before throwing them such a curveball?

It was a grueling time but as guilty as I felt, I knew in my heart that staying in my marriage would have caused more damage than leaving it. The last thing I wanted was for my sons to grow up thinking my marriage was something to be emulated. I wanted them to seek love and support and affection from a partner, and they weren't seeing that from us.

We promised them that we'd work together as a family to get through this as best as we could. We hadn't completely figured out new living arrangements. Our temporary plan was for my husband to move into the basement while he looked for a new place to live. I was going to stay in the townhouse. Eventually, I would also move, but we figured the divorce was a big enough change for the kids. We didn't want to take their home away on top of everything else.

* * *

Less than a month later, out of the blue, we got an offer on our house. It was too good to turn down, so we took it. This brought to light the fact that my husband had been borrowing money against the house to cover our expenses. As a result, we would only get a portion of the offer amount. I was livid. I was upset with him for making that kind of decision on his own, but I was angrier at myself for being naïve. I had been raised by a single mother and I knew how she struggled with finances after her divorce. I should have been more aware of what was going on in my own home.

At that moment, it dawned on me that I had never run a household or paid a bill in my entire life. When I was nineteen and first moved to Ontario, my mother took care of my rent. She had wanted to make things a little easier for me. When I got married, Nate happily took on the role of breadwinner and enjoyed being in charge. Whenever there was a form from the bank to be signed, he'd point to the line and give me a pen. No questions asked.

We sold the house. My husband settled into a condo near where my youngest went to school and I found a house close by. We had decided on a 50/50 custody split and wanted to make things as easy for the kids as possible.

My emotions at that time were all over the place. One minute I'd feel optimistic and excited for the future, and the next I'd be filled with anxiety. Several times a day, I wondered: "Holy shit! How am I going to do this?"

I wasn't afraid of being alone. I was actually looking forward to dropping my "Mrs." and being solo for a bit. It was standing on my own two feet that panicked me. Especially the finances. I had visions of being tossed out on the street for not paying my utility bills. I wasn't sure what utilities were. The sale of the townhouse had given me a bit of a safety net, but I knew it was only temporary. I was going to have to get a job. I was happy to work, but at forty-six with no degree and no valid work experience since my twenties, I wasn't a hot commodity. I needed a plan.

Once I moved into the new house, I made an appointment with a financial advisor at my bank. I sat down with a very young, very knowledgeable person who spoke incredibly quickly. I didn't understand a word she said. Words and numbers flew over my head. Every couple of minutes, I'd utter an "Uh huh" or an "Okay" to give the impression that I was following what she was saying, but it was not even close.

After the meeting, I sat in my car with a folder full of papers on my lap and cried. I felt like a complete idiot. I could feel my anxiety rising by the second. Then, surprisingly, I decided to try again.

I called the bank manager and explained what happened. He was understanding and set up an appointment for me to meet one of their senior advisors. He assured me that she'd be more patient in her approach. A few days later, I walked into the appointment feeling embarrassed and discouraged, but determined to get what I needed.

"I'm ashamed to admit this," I said as frankly as I could, "but I understand absolutely nothing about my financial situation and I need to understand *everything*. Explain things to me like I'm a child. I won't be offended."

She reached across the table and put her hand on mine. "It's okay. You're going to be okay."

She was right. This time when I left the bank, there were no tears. I felt proud of myself for being honest about my situation and getting the clarification I needed. While I was aware that I still had a lot to figure out, I was starting to feel a little more capable.

Before leaving my marriage, my therapist had described me as "a puddle of insecurity and shame with no backbone." That was about to change, and not everyone was going to be happy about it.

CHAPTER TWENTY-TWO

Dropping the Pencil

"DROP THE PENCIL!" Lana yelled at me over the phone.

Lana and I had been friends so many years ago, but we managed to reconnect after I moved back to Toronto. We quickly picked up where we left off. The only problem was that I was starting to get on her nerves with all of my self-pity and self-shaming. She told me that I started every conversation by saying, "I feel bad because . . ." I'd then proceed to criticize myself for one of my perceived imperfections. She found it frustrating. She came up with telling me to "drop the pencil" as a way to get me to stop apologizing for things that didn't require an apology.

"You feel bad about everything," she said. "You'd feel guilty if you dropped a pencil! Drop the fucking pencil, Marci!"

She was right. While I knew that leaving my marriage was the right thing to do, it left me with limited resources. I felt bad about not being in a position to give my kids everything they wanted, but my feelings of guilt went back years – way before my marriage ended. I had been overwhelmed with feelings of guilt since I was seventeen years old. I felt guilty for being alive after Billy died, guilty for battling an eating disorder, guilty for getting sick and losing a baby. I spent years feeling guilty for not being a good enough wife and still struggled with feeling inadequate as a mother.

The first year after the divorce was hard for me and hard for my kids. We all experienced the pains of adjustment and did our best to get through it. My sons were angry with me.

"You've changed," my youngest would tell me. "You're a different person now. You don't even sound the same!"

He was partially right. With every day spent away from my marriage, every new responsibility that I took on and every obstacle I overcame, I was getting stronger. But I wasn't a different person. I was just getting closer to being the person I was before I'd been stripped of my self-worth. That person was new to them. I set curfews, put limits on what I could afford to buy them, and stopped accepting behavior that was disrespectful. With every boundary I set, my spine grew back, one vertebra at a time.

For all of our screw-ups, Nate and I did one thing right. We raised two spectacular human beings who consistently made us proud. We raised them to be independent thinkers and encouraged them to speak their minds. I knew that I couldn't be angry at them for doing telling me how they felt, even if it meant they were critical of me. But I did demand that they shared their thoughts and feelings in a respectful way. Not always an easy feat for teenagers, but we were all doing our best.

We argued a lot that year. At times it was difficult to stand my ground during conflict. I didn't want them to be angry with me. I missed seeing them every day and when I did see them, I wanted our time together to be loving and fun. Setting boundaries was hard, sticking to them harder. But I did.

It was understandable that they would have trouble taking me seriously. Compared to my husband, I was a mess. Divorce is tough on both parents, but he already knew how to pay bills and had a job to go to every day. My sons watched me struggle and make a lot of mistakes as I was starting out. But every stumble I took and recovered from taught my children a valuable lesson: life is messy. If you're afraid of getting dirty, you'll miss out on amazing experiences and possibilities.

I cried my share of tears that first year. I cried to my therapist and I cried to my closest friends. I did my best to hide my sadness from my kids, but every once in a while, my oldest would sense that I was struggling. He'd surprise me with an "I love you" text or by telling me he was proud of me for doing my best. Those texts meant more to me than he'll ever understand.

Leaving a bad situation is difficult, but staying in one is worse. I left my marriage aware that things were going to be tough, but I was prepared to at least try to be tougher. I'd finally dropped the pencil.

CHAPTER TWENTY-THREE

Endure, Persist, Prevail

T'S BEEN THREE YEARS since I left my marriage. There are times I can't believe I left, but I've never questioned my decision for a second. One of the reasons that I stayed so long was I felt that it would be selfish to end my marriage just because I was miserable. I thought staying was the "right" thing. I was trying to be a good girl. "It's not *that* bad," I'd tell my friends. "It's not like he beats me."

I was right. It could have been worse, but it should have been a hell of a lot better. I had to hit so many emotional bottoms before I was ready to take the leap of faith that led me to peace and independence. I still don't have all the answers, but I don't need them. I've discovered that not knowing what's ahead of me feels strangely comforting. I see the future as full of possibility and hope. I realize that at my age most people have their lives planned, or think they have. I'm forty-nine and I don't know what I want to be when I grow up, but I'm okay with that.

I wasted too much time trying to meet other people's expectations, and I failed miserably at it. I have no idea how much time I have left on this planet, but I am going to spend all of it saying, thinking, and doing things that are genuinely right for me.

I've stopped punishing myself for the mistakes I made during my marriage. I was doing the best I could in the situations I was in. I refuse to be anchored to shame and guilt. I take the lessons I've learned and use them to propel myself forward. The truth is, I'm still making mistakes. I am now and always will be a work in progress.

Without question, the greatest gift I gave myself was forgiveness. Nobody can shame me if I'm not ashamed. Nobody can control me if I have no secrets. I've fallen madly in love with the truth. I see now that the truth won't kill me, whereas lying felt like it really might have been the end of me. I was emotionally exhausted and allowing my past to imprison me was causing actual physical pain. I needed to let the fear go.

Now that I have, I won't waste an ounce of energy pretending to be anyone other than exactly who I am. It's not always easy. For all of the "Just be yourself!" quotes circulating on social media, there is plenty of judgement towards those of us who reject or don't fit the boxes that society builds for us. It's taken me most of my life to understand that nobody has the right to make me feel insignificant, and that only I can stop that from happening.

I continue to advocate for healthy body image through my Fit vs. Fiction workshops. I'm more outspoken than ever when it comes to bashing stereotypes and debunking the unhealthy diet advice pushed on us daily. I wouldn't call myself fearless, but I no longer allow myself to drown in worries and concerns. An old friend of mine once said: "It's okay to throw yourself a pity party, as long as you know when it's time to leave." I feel my feelings, I cry my tears, and then I remind myself that whenever I thought a challenge was too hard or a hurdle too high, I proved myself wrong. I can, and I will, handle what life throws at me.

I'm dating, and still learning about myself through it. My husband met a woman a few months after we separated and has been with her ever since. That hasn't been my experience, nor would I have wanted it. I've met a lot of men in the last three years and each experience has helped me figure out what I need and want from a relationship. These lessons came in all kinds of packages: the 6′6″ nudist who lived in a trailer park and had an aversion to the truth; the arrogant foodie who spoke almost exclusively in Seinfeld quotes; the ultra-conservative gun fanatic; the narcissistic personal trainer who claimed he could beat up guys twice his size but was terrified of carbs; the newly-separated prison guard who pledged his undying love for me after our first date.

I'm not convinced there's a Mr. Right for everyone, but I'm positive that there are a lot of Mr. Wrongs, and I may have dated all of them! If I find a partner to go through the rest of my life with, that would be great. If I don't, that would be okay, too. Ending up alone doesn't scare me. The thought of being stuck with the wrong person does. After spending half my life in an unhealthy marriage, I'll be damned if I make that mistake again.

It was just a few years ago that I questioned whether or not I was strong enough to get through another day. I went from believing that I couldn't, to wondering if I could, to knowing that I can. My kids continue to see me change, and while they don't always understand the choices that I make, they respect me for making them. They call me a free spirit, and I think that's accurate.

The words *Endure, Persist, Prevail* are tattooed across my back as a guideline to getting through life's challenges. It is one of seventeen tattoos I've acquired over the last forty-nine years. Each memorializes a significant event or person in my life. Some are colorful and some are dark, like my memories. The ink on my body is a permanent reminder of the beauty that came from the strength it took to overcome my obstacles.

My body is also full of scars from the surgeries I've gone through. These are permanent as well. Where the scars brought pain and fear, my tattoos represent faith and resilience. My tattoos empower me. And my body tells my story: the good, the bad, and the very, very ugly. But it's mine, and I have finally learned to appreciate every chapter.

EPILOGUE

My Body

I've loved it
I've hated it
I've celebrated it
I've criticized it
I've abused it
I've protected it
I've trained it
I've trashed it
I've worked with it
I've worked against it
I've shared it passionately
I've shared it punishingly
I've shown it in pride
I've shown it in shame
I've fed it
I've starved it
I've created life with it
I've mourned death with it
I've endured the pain of scars with it
I've enjoyed the pleasure of tattoos with it
I've wished it were different
I've been grateful for how it is

I've fought to keep it alive
I've wondered if it was worth it
I've decided that it was
You might judge it.
People do.
You might love it
You might hate it
You might think it's too big
You might think it's too small
You might want to fuck it
You might want to friend it
You might want to ignore it completely.
It doesn't matter.
My body tells my story.
The good and the bad.
The predictable and the shocking.
The sympathetic and the scandalous.
If I invite you in, leave your judgement at the door
And be prepared to get dirty because life is messy
Oh, and wear something comfortable,
cuz there will be dancing; lots of dancing.